Horace's *Carmen Saeculare*

HORACE'S
CARMEN SAECULARE
Ritual Magic and the Poet's Art

MICHAEL C. J. PUTNAM

Yale University Press   New Haven and London

Printed in the United States of America.

Library of Congress Cataloging-in-Publication Data
Putnam, Michael C. J.
Horace's Carmen saeculare : ritual magic and the poet's art /
Michael C. J. Putnam.
p.   cm.
Includes bibliographical references (p.   ) and index.
ISBN 0-300-08333-5 (alk. paper)
1. Horace. Carmen saeculare.   2. Augustus, Emperor of Rome,
63 B.C.–14 A.D. — Art patronage.   3. Political poetry, Latin —
History and criticism.   4. Horace — Political and social views.
5. Politics and literature — Rome.   6. Rome — In literature.
7. Ritual in literature.   8. Magic in literature.   I. Title.
PA6393.C63 P88 2000
874'.01 — dc21   00-038154

A catalogue record for this book is
available from the British Library.

The paper in this book meets the guidelines
for permanence and durability of the Committee
on Production Guidelines for Book Longevity of
the Council on Library Resources.

10 9 8 7 6 5 4 3 2 1

CONTENTS

Preface

My purpose in the following book is to bring to closer critical attention one of the neglected masterpieces of the literature of Augustan Rome, Horace's *Carmen Saeculare*. In Horace's career as a lyricist the poem both stands alone, a singular song written for a singular event, and serves as transition from the first collection of three books of *Odes*, completed in 23 B.C.E., to his fourth and final volume, issued some ten years later. I came to appreciate the importance of the poem from a series of appraisals of Horace's brilliant accomplishment that began with a detailed examination of the odes of book four and continued with critiques of individual lyrics in his earlier gathering. That I single out the *Carmen* for separate treatment was urged on me by Kenneth Reckford who has been unstinting of his time, both in the sharing of ideas and in the improvement of the original manuscript. I have also benefited enormously from the readings of a later draft by Denis Feeney, who took time from a busy schedule to cast a careful eye over the whole, and by Ellen Oliensis who, as reader for Yale University Press, helped the author, in ways both general and particular, find the means to present his material more clearly and, it is hoped, more cogently.

Other friends, especially Alessandro Barchiesi, Christopher Faraone, Robert Gurval, Michael Paschalis, Matthew Santirocco, and Sarah Spence have been forthcoming with scholarly assistance in a variety of ways. I am particularly grateful to Professor Santirocco for permission to reprint some pages from "Structure and Design in Horace's *Odes* I. 17," published in *Classical World* (87 [1994]: 357–75).

The production of the manuscript was aided by Ruthann Whitten and by the computer expertise of Malcolm Hyman. I must also thank Eliza Childs of Yale University Press for her editorial care and Mary Pasti for her help in the final stages of production.

Horace's *Carmen Saeculare*

I

Introduction

The *Carmen Saeculare* is unique in the corpus of Horace's writing and in the remains of classical Latin literature because it was written for, and performed at, a public ceremony. The occasion itself was far from ordinary. In 17 B.C.E. the emperor Augustus had chosen to resuscitate, after the lapse of some one hundred and thirty years, the *Ludi Saeculares,* "games" to honor the end of one *saeculum,* defined as the span of a generous lifetime, and to initiate auspiciously the next era. The tradition of their performance was ancient, and the honor given to the poet, to write the Song that would cap the religious segment of the proceedings, therefore remarkable.

The challenge that the emperor offered Horace, and that, by accepting the invitation, the poet presented himself, was equally notable. Although the *Carmen* is Horace's only public poem, its composition marked a signal juncture in his career as lyricist, serving as transition between a Horace who, in the initial ode of his first collection, can imagine his pleasure if Maecenas, his patron and the poem's addressee, would rank him among "lyric bards" (*lyricis vatibus*) and a Horace who, in the third poem of his fourth and final gathering of odes, can identify himself as "the performer on Rome's lyre" (*Romanae fidicen lyrae*), the cynosure of his fellow citizens' eyes. The distance separating the two poems takes us from a private world of apparent interdependence between poet and patron, source of a spate of masterpieces written for contemplation, to communal acknowledgment arising from the most communal of poetic gestures. The transfer of epithet in the last quotation is purposeful. As celebrated lyricist,

Horace strums a (Greek) lyre that he has made Roman, and he does so as a Roman performing with, and before, fellow Romans during a highly conspicuous civic event.

In one detail this passage from Greece to Rome illustrates a significant intellectual hurdle that Horace set for himself here. In representing his position before Maecenas as lyric bard, the poet, by a form of metonymy as well as by the emulation apparent in his words themselves, is now adopting the stance of his most prominent intellectual forebears, the lyric poets of archaic Greece, in particular—though far from exclusively—Sappho, Alcaeus and Pindar. But at least in the first compilation of odes published in 23 B.C.E., however much he may replicate the matter and manner of his Greek predecessors, Horace feels no compulsion, nor did his contemporaries expect of him, to follow one of their primary procedures, namely the oral presentation of poetry, composed to be assimilated, at least initially, by a listening audience rather than perused by literate reader or readers.

Although the consequences of his achievement as momentarily oral bard make their mark on his subsequent verse, whether composed in lyric verse forms or in hexameters, Horace's departure in the *Carmen* from his own tradition of written poetry is unique. The resulting poem is also singular. By comparison to Horace's other hymns, which were not meant for public delivery, however exacting their references might be to the divinities addressed or to specific events in the Roman religious calendar, we sense in the *Carmen* at the very least a heightening of such rhetorical figurations as assonance and alliteration that prominently affect the aural reception of poetry. Likewise, there is more verbal repetition than is Horace's wont in his specifically written work. Such iteration not only served to help weave the poem's imaginative threads together for its original audience, but it continues to afford its hearers the pleasure of experiencing patterns of structure, be it, among other examples, through echoes that round off the poem's first half or apprise us of how beginning and end merge to create a satisfying whole. Such lexical recurrences would also function as aides-mémoire for the ode's young singers, signposts to direct their attention. Horace's use of the meter that bears Sappho's name would offer similar assistance to both performers and audience. Out of some thirteen metrical schemes utilized in his lyric corpus, Horace here chooses the most simple in form, with the quatrains' first three lines, each of eleven syllables, repeated stanza by stanza.

The ears of the participants in the ceremony, whether listeners or singers, would have found delight in the heard music of verse. The eye, which in Horace's other poetry remained the instrument for comprehension of the written word, as deployed on the page for critical appreciation, is here gratified by literally beholding the beauty of the sights depicted in the *Carmen* and by esteeming anew their importance. The audience would have watched, just as we readers still behold its ambience through the mind's inner vision, as the young chanters called attention to details of the gleaming temple to Apollo, in front of which the rites were taking place. It would have gained a greater sense of aesthetic quality and iconographic resonance of its surroundings on Rome's Palatine hill, as well as from the Aventine in the near, and the Alban mount in the far, distance.

The commissioning of the *Carmen Saeculare,* the circumstances of its creation, and its specific contents, raise the question of the poem's politics. As we will see, not only Augustus' reformulation of the *Ludi* but the ode itself paint a generously glowing picture of contemporary Rome. All things dark and dangerous are largely suppressed from Horace's praise of his world. In our present age where politics and those who profess it are equally objects of suspicion, it would be easy enough to accuse the poet of collusion with or, worse still, of public complicity in the propagandistic schemes of the emperor. The expert fiction-maker Augustus, we are prone to postulate and so the argument could run, effected this triumph of art over truth by manipulating the genius of his master-poet into fabricating one of the spiritual building blocks of his governmental enterprise. The modern reader tends to evaluate any public poem, especially one that could be charged with political bias, as second-rate. When the poet in question is Horace, whose autonomy elsewhere is notorious, and when the product of his intelligence is a virtually unalloyed eulogy of the contemporary Roman status quo, our distrust increases. We remain as wary of the poet undertaking such a venture as of the poem that is its result.

The quality of the *Carmen* itself is evidence enough to disprove such a contention or, to phrase matters more positively, to evince the poet's honest commitment to his words and their optimistic tonality. Nevertheless I would like to address such a proposition briefly from several angles. First the *Vita Horati,* the ancient life of the poet that comes down to us under the name of the biographer Suetonius, is at pains to document the emperor's deference to the poet, and not vice versa, proof that Augustus retains an awareness that immortality is often the writer's prerogative to bestow, not the politician's. Then there is the evidence of the earlier poetry. The first collection of lyrics was published eight years after Augustus' defeat of Antony at Actium had brought about both an end to a century of civil strife and his de facto establishment as sole ruler of Rome. During the intervening period, if not before, we can presume that Horace fully recognized the emperor's accomplishment and the administrative talent that lay behind it. Nevertheless, in the course of the eighty-eight brilliant odes of this gathering he could have seized the opportunity openly to praise Augustus and his works but carefully does not. In my subsequent discussion I will employ the word "conditionality" to characterize Horace's treatment therein of the chief of state. The poet imagines a series of ellipses that lay the onus of proving his quality squarely upon the emperor. Augustus will become a god if . . . ; he will be worthy of the poet's full-fledged approbation, and therefore of a share in his incantatory power, if . . . At the least we can claim for Horace that, by treating the emperor in a provisionary manner, he nudges his all-powerful subject, for all the latter's unaccountability, toward appreciation and implementation of the poet's hopes and expectations.

Then there is the evidence of the *Carmen* itself. Splendidly honorific it may be, but the ode celebrates not Augustus but the Rome that has been realized up to, and during, his regime. It is a prayer for the city, for continued protection of her patron divinities, and for the success of the emperor's own entreaties on her behalf. In fact, though elsewhere in Horace's poetry Augustus is directly named with frequency and is apostrophized in several instances, here he is only alluded to by innuendo. Although our sources universally confirm that the *princeps* called for and, we can accordingly presuppose, masterminded the festivities of which the *Carmen* forms a crucial segment, Horace draws him into the poem only as "the famous progeny of Anchises and Venus," that is, as a notable extension of tradition and described in its terms as renewer and sustainer of Rome's mythical beginnings, not as a salient entity worthy, here at least, of his own *elogium*. As a figure in the *Carmen* he is part of the continuum of Roman history just as the Song itself, and the *Ludi Saeculares* that included it, both of which modify and reinvigorate their inheritance, projecting past into future and assuring the present through the dynamism of song.

It is the Song itself, as *Carmen* and as *carmen,* that will be my primary concern in this book. After some pages on the earlier collection of odes, to establish an intellectual background within Horace's previous lyric oeuvre against which to test the Song's originality, I will examine the *Carmen,* saving a review of the intimacy of *carmina*—not only with the genre of lyric but more generally with verse's magic potential—for the book's final segment. As part of my close examination of the ode's ritual connection with "secular renewal" I will survey how the poem's patterns of repetition stand as metaphor for the religious recurrences of which it tells.

Because of the explicit logistics of the Song's performance on the Palatine on a June day in 17 B.C.E., Horace is much concerned with the specifics of its presentation and setting as well as with the more general categories of space and time. The first stretches our eye not only to Troy and its exiles arriving long ago on Italy's Tyrrhenian coast but to the bounds of modern Roman dominion, from the city's hills to the Indi in the east who bow before its sway. Space and time further interact as we trace the connection between Aeneas and Augustus, between Rome's mythic beginnings and her present bright moment of renewal. The way the poet represents his principal addressees, the gods Apollo and Diana, will also be of paramount concern. To study the first takes us both backward and forward in literature, backward to Pindar and Simonides, forward to Horace's own *c.* 4. 6, which reveals to us something of the genesis of the *Carmen* and, in particular, of aspects of Apollo's violence and penchant for vengeance that are suppressed from the Song. For the second we will look closely at Catullus poem 34, a hymn directed to the goddess, which Horace had much in mind as he wrote.

Brutality finds no place in the *Carmen;* neither does the need for apotropaic vocabulary, which elsewhere in preserved Latin letters has regular associations with the negative charm inherent in *carmina.* The voices the poet adopts, and adapts, for his own purposes are those of the Sibyl and of the Parcae (Fates), each anticipating the future, and, by implication, of Augustus, uttering his prayers as incorporated into the poet's own larger intercession before the divine. Above all we are dealing with the language of generation, which reaffirms and sustains the value and values of Rome. Such energy in turn resides in the generative power of language itself and, in the specific case of the *Carmen Saeculare* as a hymn to Rome, in the restorative powers that lie in the joyous crafting—and skilled craftiness—of words, especially as deployed with propitiousness by one of the grandest masters of lyric song.

2

Horatian Background

In the continued outpouring of books that look closely at the poet's art, the *Carmen Saeculare* of Horace remains still a neglected masterpiece. One of the reasons for this relative disregard, especially given the ode's prominent position in the Horatian corpus and in Latin letters generally, is its public nature, which allows it to be perceived as an example of political propaganda. Horace, whose independence of spirit in all his previous work, be it satires or epistles, epodes or odes, has been justly lauded, has here, such is the implication, surrendered his freedom of mind in order to write an ode manifestly in praise of contemporary Rome and, specifically, in direct glorification of the emperor, though the immediate recipients of the poem are the twin divinities Apollo and Diana who figure prominently in Augustus' remodeling of the *Ludi*. Such logic leads inevitably to the conclusion that because it is a poem which seems founded on flattery, it must be mediocre or at best a lesser manifestation of Horace's genius.

In the introduction I argued against such an assertion. In the pages that follow I will trust in the poet's honesty and support my confidence in the excellence of his work by a close reading aimed at illustrating this greatness. The *Carmen* is in fact an extraordinary example of what it would mean for Horace to write any *carmen*, a song in the hoary tradition of Roman incantation which brings about that of which it sings or, at the least, moves its readers to succumb to the charms of its expression. The difference is that in the case of the *Carmen Saeculare*, such magic potential inherent in a ritual of words, here recited, is put at the service of Rome. The poet exerts his own inner, vatic authority in order to effect externals, which in this case is to accomplish nothing less than the verbal codification and corroboration of Rome's present nobility. The city, its gods, and its leaders, salient among them the emperor himself, are the beneficiaries of the song's mesmeric potential.

Written and performed in 17, the *Carmen* is positioned near the center of the ten-year period in Horace's career that separates the publication of the first three books of odes in 23 B.C.E. and that of the final, fourth book, issued most likely in 13. There is much about the ode that anticipates the content and tone of the second collection that shortly follows. For one thing, the *Carmen* makes two appearances in the later odes. The first is implicit in the proud boast of the third poem, that the poet is ranked by Rome's populace as its supreme lyricist. Could such circumstances have arisen without the widespread notice that would have come the poet's way from his part in the *Ludi?* The second is ode 6, which, in its final stanzas, deals with the actual performance of the *Carmen* and its aftermath but as a whole has much to tell us about the ode's composition, what spurred the writer's imagination, and what he may have decided to omit from its final fashioning.

But the major repercussion of Horace's acceptance four years earlier of a public role, by writing the song that caps and concludes the central ritual of the *Ludi* as well as by directing its performance, is the continuation of largely unqualified praise for Rome and for Augustus. Four of the book's fifteen poems are devoted to the royal household and its head. Two—the fourth and fourteenth—are the closest Horace comes in his lyric career to Pindaric exuberance.[1] The first of these, exactly the same length as the *Carmen*, details the physical and moral prowess of the Nerones, Augustus' stepsons Drusus and Tiberius, against their Claudian background. The second, addressed to Augustus, is a eulogy of the two brothers whose exploits, however, redound to the credit of the emperor who lends his charisma to their undertakings.

But the balance of the two odes both in content and in positioning, as penultimate in the first and last pentads of poems that make up the book, serves one special purpose, to prepare in each instance for the poems that follow, focused now strictly on the emperor himself. In the first he is imagined as absent (the historical moment found him campaigning in the north) from a universe that yearns for him and that bears a close resemblance to that which the *Carmen* limns. The countryside is safe and productive, laws are in place that steady the people's ethics, foreign enemies are devoid of menace, and a sovereign rules for whom comparison with Hercules and Castor is not out of place because of the combination of civilizing authority that is presently his with implicit divinity that remains in store for him. In the final ode Augustus is back home and the Roman world is much the same as in poem 5, both fertile and morally upright, with enemies respectful of the city's might.

Horace is also specific in *c.* 15 about several matters that the earlier ode leaves unsaid. We are now in a post-epic era. The *Aeneid* and the fraternal strife its last books adumbrate are things of the past. As the poem explicitly puts it, the temple of Janus Quirinus is closed, bereft of battlings. (Virgil, we remember, had shown us in Jupiter's vision of a radiant Augustan future the same temple with the figure of *Furor impius*, the unholy madness of civil savagery, chained by a hundred knots.)[2] Neither *furor civilis* nor force (*vis*) nor anger (*ira*) will threaten the state's peace-inspired leisure (*otium*), which Augustus has restored.[3]

The poem's concluding mention in adjacent lines of Anchises and Venus fulfills two purposes. It reminds us of Augustus and his mythic lineage, which will continue now to be part of lyric song, not epic. It also specifically echoes line 50 of the *Carmen*, which contains the only other mention of Anchises in Horace's poetry and where once again he and his goddess paramour are juxtaposed. By recalling the emperor's ancestry as outlined in the *Carmen* in the concluding lines of his final lyric utterance, Horace intimates what the book's earlier reflections further substantiate—that the essence of the Secular Song not only abides in his last ode but will live on in the future incantations of his song.[4]

Although the fourth book of odes begins with a love poem that is one of the poet's most moving meditations on the passage of time in human lives, the transition from the *Carmen Saeculare* to the last book of odes is smooth. Whatever diverse topics the final collection may consider, Rome and its prosperous destiny under Augustus are chief among them as they are for the *Carmen*. By contrast, the passage from the first collection to the *Carmen* is anything but simple, as we watch the poet turn from the private, inner world of lyric solipsism, where even the grandest of themes is imagined as directed by the chanting "I" to virgins and boys, to the magniloquent gesture of public performance and exertion of song's magic for purposes of the state and not, at least immediately, for the delectation or cultivation of the closeted reader-hearer. Reviewing the differences between Horace's earlier lyrics and the *Carmen* makes clear the originality of the *Carmen* itself. The *Carmen*, for instance, is distinct from the earlier hymns of Horace in several salient ways. At the same time it also draws on the poet's Roman literary inheritance, primarily the works of Catullus, Virgil, and Tibullus, in a manner that differentiates it from the poet's previous lyrics. To further clarify this transition in Horace's career, I will examine here his treatment of the larger meanings of privacy in his first collection of odes, especially when it is viewed as part of the testament he establishes for himself as lyric bard.

The aloof stance of Horace's persona is visualized clearly in the sequestered landscapes in which violence, most vividly individualized in the violence of sexuality, has no part and in which eroticism itself is often sublimated. Then there is the often concomitant inner world of the poet's sacrosanctity that, because of his genius, keeps him safe from any tangible harm. However much reality enters these poems—and Augustus and Rome are already prominent presences in the troubling second ode of the first book—Horace regularly poses a distance between himself as creative artist and the immediacies of Rome as he goes about his own rituals of art-making. To renounce this posture of aloofness from which Rome can be viewed with a cool eye and accept the role of its public vindicator, with the poet unabashedly at hand in Rome, on the Palatine, performing in the company of the city's eminent, to put his gifts as vatic charmer to use not as detached, often scathing scrutinizer of the Roman political and ethical scene—his frequent posture in the initial collection—but as bardic bolsterer of her excellence, is perhaps the single most striking departure the *Carmen* takes from the first three books of odes.[5]

Beginning with *c.* 1. 17, a poem where song and setting are inextricable, I will next turn to *c.* 1. 22 on the "innocence" of the sacred bard as he chants his lyrics, no matter where, and then take up *c.* 3. 13, the famous address to the *Fons Bandusiae,* and briefly trace the symbiosis of its language and the poet's. Next I will survey how the credentials these odes establish allow Horace, in two of his most dynamic longer poems, first to ruminate before Augustus on the moderate employment of power (*c.* 3. 4) and then to offer Maecenas a meditation on the artist's self-sufficiency (*c.* 3. 29). I will then examine how the last poem of the initial grouping adopts the language of monumentality, of religion, and political power to magnify the poet's accomplishment, not to glorify the Roman establishment. I will conclude with a brief survey of the first collection's lyrics devoted to Augustus, taking particular note of their qualified nature.

First *c.* 1. 17, which I will quote in full:[6]

Velox amoenum saepe Lucretilem
mutat Lycaeo Faunus et igneam
    defendit aestatem capellis
        usque meis pluviosque ventos.

impune tutum per nemus arbutos
quaerunt latentis et thyma deviae
    olentis uxores mariti
        nec viridis metuunt colubras

nec Martialis haediliae lupos,
utcumque dulci, Tyndari, fistula
    valles et Usticae cubantis
        levia personuere saxa.

di me tuentur, dis pietas mea
et musa cordi est. hic tibi copia
    manabit ad plenum benigno
        ruris honorum opulenta cornu.

hic in reducta valle Caniculae
vitabis aestus et fide Teia
    dices laborantis in uno
        Penelopen vitreamque Circen.

hic innocentis pocula Lesbii
duces sub umbra, nec Semeleius
    cum Marte confundet Thyoneus
        proelia, nec metues protervum

suspecta Cyrum, ne male dispari
incontinentis iniciat manus
  et scindat haerentem coronam
    crinibus immeritamque vestem.

Swift Faunus often exchanges Lycaeus for lovely
Lucretilis and ever wards off fiery heat and rainy
winds from my goats. Harmlessly through the safe
wood the wandering wives of the smelly husband
search for lurking arbute and clumps of thyme, nor
do the female kids fear green vipers or the wolves
of Mars whenever, Tyndaris, the valleys and the
smooth rocks of reclining Ustica have resounded
with the sweet pipe.

The gods protect me, my piety and inspiration
are dear to the gods. Here for you from kindly horn
Abundance, rich in the glories of the countryside,
will pour forth to the full.

Here in a withdrawn valley you will avoid the
swelterings of the Dog-star and you will tell of Penelope and glassy Circe, in turmoil over one man.
Here in the shade you will quaff goblets of harmless wine from Lesbos nor will Semeleian Thyoneus
embroil battles with Mars, nor, as object of jealousy,
will you fear that forward Cyrus lay unrestrained
hands on one scarcely his equal and tear the garland
that clings to your hair and your undeserving garment.

In reading *C.* 1. 17, one of Horace's most entrancing lyrics, in
this context, I will be viewing it as central to the delineation of
his creative enterprise in the first three books of odes for its brilliant union of the depiction of landscape with the production of

poetry. To this end I will search in detail for the poetic elements that lend it such extraordinary segmental balance while at the same time generating strong forward momentum.[7] The ode is divided into seven stanzas that pivot around the central quatrain where the speaker and his guest Tyndaris, whose configuration is essential to the poem's unity, converge.[8] The gods protect the "I" of the poem and take pleasure in his piety and poetry. The "you" will copiously receive nature's abundance. Two sets of three stanzas balance each other on either side of this unifying moment. These two segments in turn have their own equilibria. It is with the first of these, lines 1–12, that I will begin.

When swift Pan trades Greece for Italy, Arcadia for the Sabine hills, and suffers a change of nomenclature from the Feeder to the Cherisher,[9] he finds himself in a landscape whose enclosing topography is echoed in the symmetrical arrangement of Horace's lines.[10] We begin and end with place names—Lucretilis and the rocks of Ustica, each mentioned only here. Within this geographical specificity, to which Horace gives authority by his act of naming, as within the enclosure of his verses, lies a magic world where both celestial and terrestrial, inanimate and animate, forms of terror are kept away from the speaker's animals. Whenever Faunus is present, summer's heat and the rainy winds of winter, that is to say, the extremes of seasonal hazards, bring no harm to the she-goats, neither do green snakes nor the wolves of Mars alarm the female kids. They are protected, free to roam without reprisal in search of arbutes and thymes.

Several details in this portrait of a charmed landscape are worth further scrutiny. First we should note one aspect of the characterization of Pan-Faunus. The etymological juncture between *Lycaeo* and *lupos* reminds us of the link between Pan and the Lupercal, the cave where the war god's wolf suckled the twin founders of Rome.[11] Horace further emphasizes the connection by adding the adjective *Martialis*. By having Faunus abandon

Mount Lycaeus and indirectly sequester Martian wolves from the poet's sacred spot, Horace has the god renounce the bestial behavior and violent sexuality implicit in the myth of the Lupercal and in the February festival that bears its name.[12]

Negative elements are banished from this pleasance. What remains within has its own special magic. Groves, arbute, and thyme, for instance, all have resonance in Horace of a landscape where delectation of body and inspiration of mind complement each other to form the poet's ideal. His only other mention of arbute occurs in the initial ode of the collection during a description of someone very like what Horace would have us imagine as partly himself, someone who breaks the day with goblets of Massic wine, lying under green arbute by a holy fountain.[13] When the speaker turns soon thereafter to the physical attributes that distinguish a poet from the mob, a chill grove (*gelidum nemus*) is conspicuous among them.[14] Likewise the only two other appearances of thyme in Horace's works both occur in analogies for a poet who pursues the sources of creativity as a bee chases after honey. The first finds Horace asking Julius Florus: "What thyme are you nimbly flying around?" (*quae circumvolitas agilis thyma?*).[15] In the second we discover Horace himself at work in his Tiburtine grove:

> . . . ego apis Matinae
> more modoque,

> grata carpentis thyma per laborem
> plurimum, circa nemus uvidique
> Tiburis ripas operosa parvos
> carmina fingo

> I, in the way and manner of a Matine bee, culling
> tasty thyme with toil on toil, around the grove and

banks of moist Tibur, in my small style I sculpt my effortful songs.[16]

The poet performs one small but telling piece of verbal sleight of hand by transferring the unexpected epithets of arbute and snake the one to the other. In his only other mention of arbute, quoted above, Horace gives it the epithet *viridis*, echoing Virgil who uses the phrase *viridis arbutus* in *ecl.* 7, a poem that Horace had much in mind as he wrote *c.* 1. 17.[17] Horace unexpectedly applies the attribute green to *colubrae*, apparently the first such designation in classical literature.[18] In an equally unwonted gesture he takes what would ordinarily be the proclivity of snakes to hide before striking—*latet anguis in herba* warns one of the protagonists of Virgil's third *eclogue*[19]—and gives it to a shrub known more usually for its color, not for any tendency toward the clandestine. In this charmed setting nature reverses her regular procedures. Goats instinctively seek, rather than shun, what is hidden, without requital, and the usually lurking snake is verbally neutralized and therefore deprived of menace by claiming for itself an attribute that both commands the attention of the eye and yet remains limited to surface description only. In this context its greenness puts the *colubra* in the same category as harmless vegetation.

Even in the behavior of the she-goats, *deviae,* wandering off their usual route, we find an analogy between the animal world and the realm of poetic imagination. I think, for instance, of *c.* 3. 25, Horace's second ode to Bacchus, which finds the lyric speaker, like Faunus here, "swift with fresh imagination" (*velox mente nova*)[20] as he is driven toward the groves and caves that are standard appurtenances for such a creative moment. Just as a Bacchante gazes mesmerized before the vista of Thrace, "so it gives me pleasure, as I wander, to marvel at river banks and empty grove" (*ut mihi devio / ripas et vacuum nemus / mirari libet*). Goats may roam scatheless in this blessed Italian arcady, but the poet, seeking his own quickening groves and sustained by metaphorical thyme, would find here the source of originality in his writing. Horace carefully distinguishes himself and his setting from Lucretius' "pathless places of the Muses" (*avia Pieridum . . . loca*).[21] His goats, and his poetry, do not aim for trackless spots but for mental areas different from the ordinary taken by the less gifted. His specialness comes from comparison with the straightened intellectual circumstances of others, not (here at least) from claims of uniqueness.

There are men in this world. Faunus arrives, the (presumably) masculine speaker possesses his flock, the goat-wives have a smelly husband. But aside from these three individual male characters, all the inhabitants of this sacred space are groups of female animals, the *capellae,* the *haediliae,* and, in between, those *deviae uxores.* It is the wives who are at liberty to wander at will while Faunus deflects meteorological danger from the she-goats and the female kids sense no threat from wolf or snake. In other words, the majority of the denizens with which Horace peoples his landscape are female, and it is specifically from them that terror is isolated and for them that safety and freedom from requital are assured.

The topography itself is also carefully feminized. There is no exact parallel for the Latin phrase *Usticae cubantis,* for a hillside that "reclines," as if in illness, or at ease, or during a sexual encounter. The resulting personification slips over into the phrase *levia saxa* as well. Ustica's rocks are smooth, to aid in the resounding echo that they produce, but in this context their smoothness is a further reference to a woman's body at its ease. We think, for instance, of Catullus' mention of the smooth arms (*levia bracchia*) of Ariadne[22] or Virgil's of Amata's smooth breast (*levia pectora*).[23] This powerful feminization of the second landmark that Horace chooses to name helps to bracket it neatly with *amoenum Lucretilem,* the initial mountain he identifies. It is common enough in Latin literature to label a landscape or its constituent parts—shrubs, fields, roses—as *amoenus,* pleasant to the senses. But the link of the adjective here with *cubantis* and *levia* adds a further level of eroticism that verges on personification.

It is into this suggestive setting that Horace's speaker invites Tyndaris, fashioning her, through the brilliant phrase *dulci, Tyndari, fistula,* into a synecdoche of the larger landscape itself. Assonance and further vocalic repetition meld the words together, at once surrounding Tyndaris and merging her with the sweetness of the panpipes. But this enclosure, with its own particularized resonance, is but a microcosm of the larger precinct into which it is set, a precinct verbally mimicked in the balanced place names that bound the opening three stanzas and gifted with the larger reverberation of hill with hill which the music of the pipe provokes.

Horace configures his final three stanzas with a parallel act of framing. At the same time he is at pains to maintain continuity between the poem's major segments. Our first meeting with Tyndaris occurs as *valles* reecho with the sound of the syrinx. As we move from the doings of animals to the activities of humankind and as Tyndaris and, vicariously, the speaker take over the poem, we turn from a general to a particular setting. He locates his guest *in reducta valle,* in a withdrawn valley, a place, if we can judge from Virgil's two uses of the phrase, at once mysterious and inspirational where, in Aeneas' case, the hero is twice-over initiated into his future.[24] This equally solemn moment in Horace's lyric world imparts its own sense of ceremony to Tyndaris' role in what follows.

Meanwhile the opening of the poem is not forgotten as Horace elaborates the particulars of his invitee's world apart. Initially, Faunus wards off fiery heat (*igneam aestatem*) and rainy winds from the speaker's goats. Now the speaker can pronounce that "you will avoid the sweltering heat of the Dog-star" (*Caniculae vitabis aestus*). Animals and man are both ordinarily subject to elemental nature and in each case we enter into their realms with the pronouncement that the perils that nature regularly offers will now be held at bay or avoided. But there is a subtle difference between *aestatem* and *aestus*, which in turn prepares us for the change from the world of goats to the domain of men. The meaning of *aestas* is essentially restricted to summer heat. *Aestus*, however, carries further metaphorical associations with human emotionality, whether the passion be love or fury. Although here directly associated with the torridness of Sirius, *aestus* hints as well at what is to come as the poem evolves toward its conclusion.[25] As we turn from animal to man and to the addition of poetry to the sound of music, it is not snakes and wolves that must be shunned but the violence that Bacchus and Mars together might bring to the *convivium*. The importunate ardor of Cyrus must especially be prohibited entry. Once more the wolfish war god must be excluded, but Cyrus, too, is a bestial figure. His incipient amatory impetuosity balances, and absorbs, the "passions" of nature, and together they form the poetic bounds of the poem's second half.

As figures whether natural, allegorical, or human, Mars, Bacchus, and Cyrus are eliminated from the charmed moment of song, wine, and shade, but their mention as part of its definition keeps their ominous presence before us. The metronymics Semeleius and Thyoneus, which distinguish Bacchus, offer a case in point. It has been observed that "Horace is not wholly serious in accumulating these *eponymiai*,"[26] but he does have at least one purpose that is highly apropos. From the many options in Bacchus' nomenclature, Horace chooses two connected with a woman, Semele, the god's mother. The first reminds us of her history, blasted by the thunder and lightning of Zeus while she was pregnant with her son. The second recalls the psychic phenomenon that she was driven to maddened fury, a characteristic to which her son was to lay claim in a more active manner. The speaker offers only harmless wine to Tyndaris in this safe haven. The aspects of Bacchus' nature that destroy a woman or drive her to fury, the *aestus* of human emotionality, are relegated elsewhere.

Then there is the figure of Cyrus. He appears in two guises during the course of the *Odes*. In *c.* 1. 33 he seems, as he does in *c.* 1. 17, lyric's or elegy's standard lover; in the first, pined for by a girl while he desires another, here unable to manifest the rage to which his jealousy might give rise.[27] We have also the historical Cyrus of Horace's greatest symposiastic ode, *c.* 3. 29. It is not now amatory impetuosity that threatens the *convivium* that Horace offers Maecenas (presumably) at his Sabine farm but the larger worries posed for the state by eastern enemies, such as Scythia or "Bactra reigned over by Cyrus" (*regnata Cyro Bactra*), which is to say Parthia.[28] But the historical Cyrus may be vicariously present in *c.* 1. 17 through his modern namesake. It was after all the Achaemenid emperor who, in the mid-sixth century B.C.E., drove Anacreon and his fellow citizens away from Teos in Asia Minor to found Abdera in Thrace. No such peril would alarm Tyndaris from a later Cyrus should she, as Anacreon *rediviva,* sing on Teian lyre in the safe shelter of Horace's Sabine retreat.

The ode moves with ease from the animal world to the human, from goats protected as they forage in a landscape that resounds with the pipe of Pan to Tyndaris in the shade, singing and drinking wine. But, as we have seen, there is sufficient overlap between the initial triad of stanzas and the last three, fostered by verbal repetition and parallelism of structure, to suggest that the subjects of the two groupings are to a degree analogous, especially when the intervening central stanza is included in the survey. The setting is in each case a valley (11, 17) where summer heat (8, 24) is problematic. It offers safety to its denizens (*tutum*, 5; *tuentur*, 13), freedom from fear (8, 24) and in particular from the menace of Mars (9, 23). In each case enemies are eliminated (*defendit*, 3; *proelia*, 24) and lack of retribution in the animal world (*impune*, 5) finds correspondence in the harmless wine (*innocentis*, 21) that Tyndaris will drink or in her undeserving garment (*immeritam*, 28), personified like reclining Ustica, which Cyrus will not tear.[29] The commonality of music needs no further comment.[30]

But there is also one very Horatian aspect to the *convivium* to which the speaker briefly alludes and which will help us discover a still deeper level of congruity running through the poem. This revolves around the notion of parity. Horace touches on it only glancingly—and negatively—when he mentions the uncontrollable hands that Cyrus will not be able to lay on Tyndaris, someone who is *male dispari*, distinctly ill suited to him. The same negative view of parity recurs in Horace's final symposiastic ode, *c.* 4. 11, where Phyllis is invited by the speaker to share his celebration for the birthday of Maecenas, to learn to sing his songs back to him, and to give up pursuing Telephus who is *dispar*, as unlike her as presumably the speaker is akin.[31]

Horace puts his thoughts more positively in *epistles* 1. 5, an invitation to Torquatus to be his *conviva* and stretch out the summer night with good conversation. The core of this exceptional poem is a definition of the dynamics as well as of the consequences of wine-drinking. Among the demands the speaker as host places upon himself to achieve a setting as suitable as possible for his guests are: that the tankard and plate show "you to yourself," "that there be no one among faithful friends to carry abroad what is spoken" (*ne fidos inter amicos/sit qui dicta foras eliminet*),[32] and, in place of climax, "that like may meet and join with like" (*ut coeat par/iungaturque pari*).[33] On applying this dictum to the circumstances of *c.* 1. 17, we appreciate directly that he who is *dispar,* in this case headstrong Cyrus, has been banned from the proceedings. The question of parity, of equality and balance, between Tyndaris and the variegated conditions in which she would find herself were she to accept the speaker's invitation, is left unexplored, but its implications are by innuendo operative throughout the poem and, by the very fact of being unstated, serve as the ode's most artful means of enchantment.

Tyndaris would hear of herself, which is to say see herself in her mind's eye, mirrored in the inanimate landscape, lovely and smooth, and yet through *cubantis* suddenly come alive to anticipate proleptically her posture at the *convivium* or perhaps even her role as an *hetaira.* She would listen to the sound of the panpipes and observe the symbolic aspects of grove, arbute, and thyme, finding in both activities inspiration for, and complementarity with, her own music-making. As for the creatures who animate this charmed spot, the ones who are specifically sequestered from fear are all female, like Tyndaris herself who, should she venture into the speaker's world, need not fear Cyrus' brutality. Perhaps, too, these wives of the smelly he-goat, who wander from the beaten path without retribution, are even meant to offer a homely analogy for the subject of her future song, Circe and Penelope "laboring" for Odysseus, two women in love with one man.

But the subtlest form of parity lies between Tyndaris and the speaker and works on several levels at once. Most obviously, both share in the symposium. She drinks his wine and wears the *corona* that adorns each participant. A deeper intimacy lies in the fact that both are poet-singers. She will sing to him in the manner of Anacreon. He will offer in return the "wine" of Lesbos, which for Horace means poetry in the manner of Sappho and Alcaeus, beginning with this very ode written in the latter's meter.[34] He has just boasted that his muse, his poetic skill and accomplishment, is dear to the gods, but suddenly we have Tyndaris doing what we might expect "Horace" to do, namely, to sing love songs in the shade. On still another level she is parallel to Quintus Horatius Flaccus. She is made to create poetry after a pattern set by Anacreon, and yet several of Horace's most anacreontic poems—I think particularly of *c.* 1. 23 and 1. 27— follow shortly in the collection of lyrics.[35] Within the imagined world of the poem she is on a par with the poet, one compatible singer schooled in earlier Greek lyric singing to another, their accomplishments parallel to each other. When we step outside the poem to analyze influences, she becomes Horace himself, singing now, and soon again, in Teian mode. She is both the product and the exemplification of his muse, *par* to him in the deepest sense.[36]

Study of such a complementarity leads to the question of the poem's originality, one aspect of which has particular bearing here. When Horace has Tyndaris sing of Penelope and Circe in love with Odysseus, he is having her patently break new ground. The *Anacreonta* never use mythological subjects and Anacreon himself explicitly avoids such material as potentially unsettling at a banquet.[37] Epic and lyric as genres, Homer's myths, and Anacreon's hedonistic elegant immediacy are, in their different ways, incompatible with each other. Horace's speaker underscores, and honors, this unprecedentedness with one detail in the last stanza, namely, Tyndaris' *haerentem coronam,* the crown that clings to her hair, which Cyrus cannot rend. This is the conviviast's garland, but in this context it is also the poet's crown, which easily shades into the crown of poetry, the imaginative "garland" that elicits the tangible emblem of accomplishment. But the phrase *haerentem coronam* is of special importance. Horace had used it earlier, in *sat.* 1. 10, where the context sheds light on its reappearance in the present ode:

> ... neque ego illi detrahere ausim
> haerentem capiti cum multa laude coronam.[38]

> nor would I dare wrest from his head the crown that
> clings with great praise.

Horace is looking to the past history of satire and acknowledging that he would not attempt to rival his great predecessor Lucilius, certainly not to the point of claiming any superiority to him. The crown of poetic originality still clings to Lucilius' brow as it does to the locks of Tyndaris, Anacreontic singer imagined into being by Horace to expand the potential of Teian song. Her crown is part of the "history" of the poem, awarded for originality as poet-singer for the speaker's *convivium*.[39] It is one ode's small version of the Delphic laurel with which Horace orders Melpomene to gird his locks as he brings his lyric masterpiece to a close.[40]

In my discussion I have come close, as one always tends to do with Horace, to equating the speaker with the creative mind behind his words. This identification becomes particularly cogent when the topic is the ode's intellectual background and the manipulation of genres that we are meant to sense in its composition. What is beyond argument is the kinship, based on exactly these grounds, that Horace manufactures between his speaker, who accommodates elements of pastoral and didactic poetry to lyric while barring elegy, and the ode's invitee, who in her turn, at least according to his imagination of her, will reduce epic grandeur to a tale of female eroticism and to a role as divertissement at a *convivium*. This further suggestion of compatibility between speaker and guest hints again at their potential union in more human terms.

In other words, the speaker's awareness of Tyndaris' multifaceted talent and of its parallels to his, which the poem would make abundantly obvious to her, insinuates once more that the poem itself is an act of seduction, the powerful signal that the beautiful new Helen would find herself in sympathy with what she found if, like Pan become Faunus, she transferred herself to the extraordinary surroundings of Horace's Sabine setting. For Tyndaris-Helen, this topographical relocation connotes one further mutation from epic to lyric as Horace co-opts and tames to his own lyric purposes the figure who, more than any other in Homer, fuses eroticism with war's violence. Helen's adaptation to Horace's odic world thus transforms her from a cause of violence into someone from whom fury is kept at a distance, from a weaver of the deeds of war that she both instigates and witnesses into a singer whose task is to modify and delimit her Homeric inheritance.

Continuing the survey of the theme of the poet's magic and its connection both with landscape and with his sacrosanctity along with the special potency of lyric per se, let us turn to *c*. 1. 22, a poem that has much in common with the Tyndaris ode. But if the pastoral oasis of *c*. 1. 17 symbolizes the shelter Horace offers his guests, *c*. 1. 22 dwells on the invulnerability of the poet in whatever topography he is placed. In *c*. 1. 17 the safety of animals and humans in Horace's hidden valley is assured against both inanimate or living menace, be it emanating from the threatening heat of the Dog-star or from the potential sexual violence that Cyrus might offer. Horace may be luring Tyndaris into his secluded world for amatory purposes, but it is her connection with poetry that is paramount. She sings the eroticism of the *Odyssey* the way an Anacreon would, but she is also Helen, beautiful seductress to be sure but also the subject of Homer's epic and a second Homer within that poem as she weaves on a tapestry what Homer sings in verse. Horace thus becomes a latter-day Homer or, better, a Roman Anacreon who lyricizes Homer, and Helen is both object of his song and singer within it. He accomplishes for Tyndaris/Helen what Tyndaris/Anacreon does for Penelope and Circe. Given the amount of allusivity in the poem that complements her presence, she appears a type of muse about to perform before us, an incorporation of the speaker's inner imagination that is as dear to the gods as his holiness. She inspires one of Horace's most astonishingly beautiful poems, as he sings of her potential song.

No wolves threaten Horace's kids in *c.* 1. 17, nor does the portentous *lupus* of *c.* 1. 22 bring him any harm. The physical, however monstrous, cannot touch the embodiment of spiritual genius. But now we are in a different landscape. In *c.* 1. 17 the she-goats are *deviae,* capable of wandering unhurt where they would. Yet they are shielded from trial only within the specific, named locale of Lucretilis and Ustica, which is to say within the protected environment of the poet's muse. In *c.* 1. 22 the speaker embodies within himself the immunity that landscape offers in *c.* 1. 17, as he is envisioned wandering *ultra terminum,* beyond the bounds past which ordinary mortals should dare not venture. If valley and muse defend the inhabitants of the inspiring *locus amoenus* against, say, the "swirlings of the Dog-star" (*Caniculae aestus*), it is his own internal potency as holy, enchanting *vatis* that keeps the speaker inviolable against the threats that the extremes of topography might bring, be they the "swirling Syrtis" (*Syrtis aestuosas*) or the Caucasus that has no liking for guests.

But there are essential items shared by the two poems, chief of which is the commonality of music, song, and poetry. Tyndaris easily shades into Lalage, the addressee of the later lyric, and the implicit sexuality of *c.* 1. 17 becomes the explicit announcement of *c.* 1. 22: "I will love" (*amabo*). The singer who in *c.* 1. 17 elicits Horace's graceful song becomes in *c.* 1. 22 the girl who is object of that song (*canto*). It is presumably a combination of the bard's spiritual uprightness and the quality of his utterance that preserves him as he tells of her, no matter how challenging the circumstances. The purport of that utterance is no doubt a love song, but it is certainly also directed toward song in and of itself. The name "Lalage" means she who prattles, an etymology that Horace calls directly to our attention by telling us of the sweetness of her talk (*dulce loquentem*), the poem's final line.

Allusion also plays a crucial part in interpretation here. Any reader looking at the concluding verses—

> dulce ridentem Lalagen amabo,
>   dulce loquentem.

> I will love Lalage, laughing sweetly, talking sweetly.

—would think of Catullus' address to Lesbia as *dulce ridentem*.[41] This bow to Horace's immediate poetic past in turn takes us back to archaic Greece and to Sappho 31, of which the Catullan poem is a translation, and to the girl there "laughing longingly" (γελαίσας ἱμέροεν)[42] at the man opposite her. But if Lalage is in part Lesbia, she is also specifically the girl in Sappho's poem. Lesbia laughs but she doesn't speak. Sappho's cynosure by contrast not only laughs, she also "speaks sweetly" (ἆδυ φωνείσας) as does Lalage.[43] So by etymology, by allusion, and by positioning Horace gives special stress to the speaker who talks sweetly.

References in the poem to Catullus (and there are several more) and to Sappho, as well as the fact that Horace invents in song a female speaker whose talking brings the poem to a conclusion that also suggests continuation, together propose a communion of ideas not dissimilar to that which the poet creates in *c*. 1. 17. Lalage, like Tyndaris, is a love object, but she is also a center for poetry. To sing of her "sweetly speaking" is to tell of her also as a muse, as inspiring as she is inspired. She also brings with her Catullus and Sappho, that is to say the lyric tradition stretching from the preceding generation in Roman letters back to the genre's initial practitioners in early Greece. So once again lyric song and the poet's creation of a singer, who also serves as muse, are important components of a sheltered world, in the case of *c.* 1. 17, of a landscape that both shields and inspires, in that of *c.* 1. 22, of the inventing poet himself whose imagination and its outpourings take Lalage, the love of lyric and its creation, with him as protective, spiritual armor against all hazards.

Another ode that varies these same themes is the beautiful address to the *fons Bandusiae, c.* 3. 13.[44] This poem deals with a pastoral oasis, now at least superficially in more literal form. Like the landscape of *c.* 1. 17 with its she-goats and kids, the *fons* provides refreshment for a "wandering flock" (*pecori vago*). Our fountain is also a haven for denizens of the georgic world as well, "bulls tired from the share" (*fessis vomere tauris*). Here, too, a threatening exterior sphere is warded off from the poet's magic spot. "The ferocious season of the Dog-star" (*atrox hora Caniculae*) can no more affect those refreshed by the spring's waters than the "swirlings of the Dog-star" (*Caniculae aestus*) can those who, like Tyndaris, share in the poet's mesmeric country space.

Here, however, Horace conceives for us a sacred spot where, unlike the landscape of *c.* 1. 17 whither Tyndaris is to be welcomed or the speaker's inner imagination as suggested in *c* 1. 22, which ever dwells on Lalage and song no matter how extreme the physical environment, sexuality in any guise is unwelcome. First, there is the goat whose red blood, as part of tomorrow's sacrifice, mingling with the spring's chill streams has offended critics.[45] Goat and fountain are nearly mirror images, *fons* echoed in *frons*. Yet the fountain is as gleaming and artistically still as glass, the goat's brow tumescent with horns, ready to prove its valiance in love's battles and its appropriateness as symbol for lustiness. The adjective *turgidus* (14) is brilliantly chosen as merging both realms. The forehead of the goat is swollen, the way a stream might become under different meteorological circumstances but our calm *fons* could never be. But in the case of the goat we sense the early stages of a sexual excitement that is foreign to the fountain's fortune.

Lucretius uses similar vocabulary in a vivid description of sexual arousal and, in particular, of "places swollen with much seed" (*loca turgida semine molto*).[46] He follows this detail with a graphic equation of semen with *sanguis* and *ruber umor*.[47] For Horace, just as *turgidus* joins water and brow through the image of sexual stirring, so *rubro sanguine* (7) sublimates any direct association of sexual energy by changing its suggestiveness into the blood of sacrifice that is ritually absorbed by the fountain. Red is counterbalanced not by an expected white but by chill, as a word of visual perception yields to one of tactility. But it is a tangibility that on a physical level cannot expect—indeed doesn't desire—any response. In such a metaphoric context the verses *te flagrantis atrox hora Caniculae / nescit tangere* ("the ferocious season of the Dog-star doesn't know how to touch you," 9–10) take on added significance. Sirius stands not only for the heat of high summer when animals most urgently need the renewal offered by water and shade. The threat that the Dog-star poses to the fountains, through the intimations of the participle *flagrans*, turns atmospheric warmth into the burning of amatory desire. The personified *atrox hora* wants to bring its blighting force to the fountain but doesn't know how. It cannot "touch" the fountain, which is to say it cannot literally bring withering heat to the spring or, metaphorically, devirginate it with its eager touch.

We are left with the paradox of *frigus amabile* (10). The fountain as a nourisher of its environment tenders a love that is properly assuaging of the summer heat, but as a lover herself she remains antonymically chill to the goat's "hot blood" or to the ardent fierceness of Sirius.

But there is another aspect of love that is central to the poem's meaning. As its first line tells us, the fountain is *splendidior vitro,* "more gleaming than glass." This is to say that it is reflective, that it gives us back an image, of ourselves should we take advantage of that feature of its beauty. But this mutuality, with its intimations of self-discovery, reveals its full potential only in the poem's last stanza. There we learn that the fountain does in fact have a relationship built on a pivotal interdependence. The speaking "I," which here as often we come near equating with Horace himself, has the power in words to ennoble the fountain (*me dicente*), that is, as many critics have pointed out, to raise this Italian source to the level of those in Greece, such as Castalia or Hippocrene, that have served as seats of the Muses and therefore as sources of inspiration for poets.

But the speaker of the poem has particular reason to execute this task because of what the fountain has already presented to him. It is active as well as passive. From one angle it is the creature of a poet who has the ability to conjure into being a source, like the fountains of Greece, with the potential of prodding the imagination of subsequent poets, presumably, as well as of himself. It stands, in other words, for the poetry of Horace in its role of muse for future bards. But it also remains his inspiration and stimulus. In its role as resplendent surface, the personified spring grants the poet the material of his trade, with "speaking waters" (*loquaces lymphae*) that stimulate him to raise his own native spring to the level of muse, telling of what he has been told.

As in *c*. 1. 22, Horace has again drawn deeply on Catullus. For one example, the personified waters, leaping and chattering, look back to the earlier poet's *phaselus*. This little boat began life as woods that gave forth a whistling from its "talking foliage" (*loquente coma*),[48] but its characteristic ability to talk stayed with it as, even now, the poem's speaker recalls its continued recounting of its story to visitors who marvel at its adventures. But the fountain's even closer cousin is the poet's own Lalage, *dulce ridentem . . . , dulce loquentem.* Lalage stands for the poet's muse as well as for his lyric tradition, the source of his inspiration and his originality. She is the subject and the object of his song. She is also the expression of the vatic holiness that keeps him sacrosanct, spiritually whole, whatever physical challenges he might have to confront. His voice, here of love songs for Lalage, is the instrument that chants *carmina* both shielding and charming, warding off the malign but likewise effecting the tangible by the intangible, by the utterance of a ritual of words that accomplishes the deeds with which it is concerned. It is after all song and the act of singing that save the speaker from external harm (9–12):

> namque me silva lupus in Sabina,
> dum meam canto Lalagen et ultra
> terminum curis vagor expeditis,
>   fugit inermem, . . .

> for while I keep on singing my Lalage and wander
> beyond the bounds, free of worries, a wolf in the
> Sabine wood fled me unarmed,

The stable inner world that the speaker takes with him on his journey of Lalage-song finds a topographical complement in the *fons Bandusiae.* Its talking waters (*loquaces lymphae*) are the counterpart of Lalage *dulce loquentem.* The fountain is at once still and in motion, possessed of the shimmer of glass and yet with leaping waters as well. Its spatiality thus partakes in both the horizontal and the vertical, with the resplendent bowl of the spring receiving the streams as they fall, and with the ilex tree and the hollow rocks further marking both qualities. Yet, for all the attributes that give it distinction, the *fons* is immobile, like the poet's sequestered valley in *c.* 1. 17, with its hallowed poet and its muse, that thrusts away both meteorological and human violence. The fountain is a center and a source, worthy of ritual sacrifice and of the rhetoric of hymnic apostrophe that glorifies its sanctity with wine, flowers, and animal sacrifice. It lures to itself and sustains flocks and poet alike, the bodies of nature's fauna and the mind of a singer of songs.

In these three odes we survey examples of how the poet defines his muse. Landscape is often an essential ingredient in the formulation. In *c.* 1. 17 and 3. 13 valley and fountain function as locales apart, which determine the private, exclusive world of song-making. In *c.* 1. 22 the poet in his Sabine woods departs from the safety of his Terminus' bounds but brings with him an interior realm of such integrity and magnetism that its exterior manifestation, in the act of song, can, Orpheus-like, tame the wild and render powerless any outward threats against its possessor.

In all three cases we find a speaker living in the country—not the city—finding inspiration from and within his retreat, which stands as metaphor for his life of the mind, and remaining remote from the responsibilities that allegiance to a civic existence entails, namely, a direct concern with politics and, in particular, with any social obligations as the greatest lyric genius of Augustan Rome. When these spheres come into collision, their friction creates some of Horace's most extraordinary poetry. I would like to look briefly at two examples. The first is the fourth of the sextet of poems, the so-called Roman odes, that open the third book of *Carmina*. It is distinguished for being the longest of Horace's lyrics and the central of three poems that have Augustus as a major subject of consideration. I will return shortly to the other mentions of the emperor in poems 3 and 5. Here I would like to watch how *c.* 3. 4 expands on elements I have been tracing in the poems that deal with Horace's vatic vocation and its sources and how politics enter the picture to make the ode central to my discussion.

The ode begins with an address to Calliope, muse of lovely sound, to descend and tell, through the poet, an extended bout of song (*longum melos*). Then suddenly the speaker becomes a dreaming "I," the plaything of loving madness (*amabilis insania*), wandering among holy groves (*pios lucos*) suffused with lovely waters and breezes.[49] Then, with an equal briskness, we find ourselves following the miraculous fortunes of the speaker as young child who when he wandered "beyond the boundaries of his nurse Pullia" (*nutricis extra limina Pulliae*) was covered with foliage by Venus' doves, left unharmed by vipers and bears, and surrounded by the symbolic laurel and myrtle of the burgeoning bard.[50] This holy inviolability has a present, past, and future. It remains his protective guard whether in the Sabine country, at cool Praeneste or Tibur, or at clear Baiae (no mention here of Rome either for living or for composing).[51] It preserved him from harm at specific moments in his human biography, at Philippi, from the fall of a tree or from shipwreck. The Muses' custody will keep him safe no matter what outer menace might come his way from any variation of experience, be it posed by the maddened Bosphorus, Assyria's burning sands, the Britons ferocious to guests (*hospitibus feros*), or the Concanus who barbarically delights in the blood of horses. Then, to round out the poem's first half, we return to the Muses, now bringing refreshment to Caesar in their Pierian cave, once war is past and the emperor's veterans are settled.

Horace initiates the ode's second segment with another address, now not just to the specific muse of *melos* but to all the sisterhood as *almae*, nourishing purveyors of *lene consilium*, counsel that is based on gentleness (*lenitas*).[52] The "counsel" follows in the speaker-poet's words. "You give," he says of the Muses; "we know" he forthwith applies to himself and his inspirers conjoined together—an expansion of the "you" and "I" that mark the poem's initial quatrains. What "we know" takes up the poem's final forty lines and consists in a magnified lyric evaluation of an epic, mythological event, the confrontation of Olympian gods with giants and titans. We are dealing with force against force, but the one side relies on impiety, corporeal hugeness, and the bold brutalness of physicality; the other consists, among others, of Jupiter, mother Juno, and an Apollo who never puts bow aside yet also washes his hair in "the pure dew of Castalia." He is a war god but also the god of Delphi's spring, patron of music, prophecy, and their combination in the vatic poet's art.

In the midst of the adventure the speaker offers a moral (65–68):

> vis consili expers mole ruit sua,
> vim temperatam di quoque provehunt
>   in maius, idem odere viris
>   omne nefas animo moventis.

> Force lacking counsel collapses by its own mass, force that is tempered the gods themselves convey to greater things, equally they loath force that prompts every evil with its animus.

Three appearances of *vis,* the first two in anaphora, shape the stanza. The first and third define the negative use of force—lacking counsel and therefore prone to causing its own ruin or engendering criminality by its own savage strength. The gods, whose civilizing rationality wins the conflict, approve the mean course where *vis* and *temperantia,* energy and restraint, operate together. We presume that the *consilium,* which the first, malign recourse to force is lacking, joins *temperantia* to decide the proper application of human energy, especially in military matters, which exerts itself under the control of moderation and judicious wisdom.

We have already been offered an example of such conduct in

the realm of the immortals, not in the person of Apollo but in that of the king of the gods himself (45–48):

> qui terram inertem, qui mare temperat
> ventosum et urbis regnaque tristia,
>   divosque mortalisque turmas
>   imperio regit unus aequo.

> who calms the rooted earth, calms the wind-tossed
> sea and cities and the kingdom of sadness, and who
> peerless rules the gods and mortal throngs with bal-
> anced rule.

Although his *imperium* is absolute, Jupiter commands his universe with a potency known, again, for *temperantia* as well as *aequitas* and therefore combining prudence and balance in its employment.

The intimations of allegory in this extended homily would not have been lost on the human but potentially epiphanic equivalent of the king of the gods, Augustus himself, who can now settle his victorious troops and receive the Muses' sustenance again. The crucial battle of Actium is over, untrammeled wickedness has been defeated and, with brutish opposition rendered powerless, civil war is only a memory. But with triumph comes responsibility, especially in employing the sovereignty attached to singular rule with sagacity and discretion. This means that Augustus, if we follow out Horace's suggestiveness, must be both Jupiter and Apollo at once, charged now with duties concomitant with one-man reign yet capable of putting away the bow and listening to the Muses. This is obliquely to say that he must now attend, in general, to the life of the spirit and, in particular, to his poet and to the proleptic guidance his thoughtful words provide.

Horace can purvey this education by the Muses because of the intellectual setting he establishes for himself in the first half of the poem. And though in the ode's second segment he embarks on one of his grandest statements about the ethics of political governance, he does so from a position of independence where external attributes are symbolic reflections of the mind's inner prowess. These signs smack of the setting we earlier traced in *c.* 1. 17, 1. 22, and 3. 13 and combine characteristics that in the shorter lyrics are often separate. Tracing parallels to the Bandusian spring, we find the holy groves amid which lovely waters course, and among places where the speaker acknowledges his possession by the Muses, we find the steep Sabine hills, cool (*frigidum*) Praeneste, and clear Baiae. The Sabines are the setting for the sequestered valley of *c.* 1. 17, and it is from the confines of the Sabine woods that, in *c.* 1. 22, the invulnerable poet wanders abroad. Cool Praeneste reminds us of the fountain's *frigus amabile,* and Baiae's limpid waters recall the spring's lambent streams that the goat's blood will stain.

The sacrosanctity of the poet, which *c.* 1. 22 illustrates, is also a major concern at the opening of *c.* 3. 4. On this occasion a wolf is replaced by vipers and bears, and the places in which *c.* 1. 22 locates the wandering speaker, as he imagines himself experiencing the extremes of hot and cold, gain both detail and specificity in the catalogue of *c.* 3. 4. 29–36. But there is one major difference in the two portraits of the bard's inviolability. In *c.* 1. 22 the poet roams beyond the terminus of his Sabine abode. In *c.* 3. 4 it is outside the "threshold of his fabled nurse Pullia" that he strays unscathed. We are now meant to imagine a time some thirty years before the Sabine hills became focal to the poet's imaginative life and a place three hundred kilometers southeast of Rome as the crow flies. We are witnesses to the poet's birth and early life and therefore to the fact that the protection of the Muses began at the start of his curriculum vitae and continues to stay with him, and to sustain him, whatever the hazards that he has confronted or that might remain in store in life, especially as he fulfills the responsibilities of his Apolline vocation.

Recounting the poet's literal and spiritual biography, his invulnerability as vatic singer, and the sources of his imagination's brilliance, therefore, takes up a share of this grand ode equal to that devoted to scanning the mythic conflict of gods against giants and titans, and to intimating its modern analogy.[53] The credentials to lecture the warrior are as important as the lecture itself. And in suggesting that the man of power should attend now to the goddesses of art, Horace does not so much put his gifts at the service of the public world of political and martial energies as lure that world into his own museful existence. For Augustus to learn what "we know" is to become part of that imaginative aesthetic and, now that war is over, to share not in some physical invincibility, which a god might utilize against the violence of his enemies especially in acts of retaliation, but in the life of the spirit, as practiced in a Sabine valley or at an inspiring fountain whence poetry springs.

As a whole, therefore, the ode looks essentially at Horace's inner life and at how it is of value to those who rule the state, should they be percipient enough to fall under its spell. The public world is at the mercy of the private. Those who gain, and hold, their positions by physical force or use it in implementing their aims, even when these ends are laudatory, can only learn proper comportment from others who, in several senses, rest apart from the center of power. Seclusion, as metaphoric category for his spiritual life, fosters the poet's ability to direct the comportment of the highest political officials. Just as the Sabine farm and the Bandusian spring are topographically distant from Rome and its concentration of governmental authority, so the poet's vocation as vatic singer of magic *carmina* sets him apart from ordinary mortals in that he is not subject to anything minatory in whatever physical environment he finds himself. It is in Horace's mental world, in his imagination, especially as empowered to educate, that *c.* 3. 4 urges Augustus to dwell.

The same notion is varied in the brilliant penultimate ode of the collection, *c.* 3. 29, but this time the addressee is Maecenas who straddles the two spheres—confidant of Augustus yet patron of poets, dweller in Rome yet bestower on Horace of his Sabine estate and therefore aware, we may trust, of its multivalent meaning. The ode serves as invitation to the statesman, proposing that he abandon the "smoke, commercialism, and noise of wealthy Rome" and join "Horace" for wine, roses, and essence of balsam that have long been reserved for him.[54] There is no need now for an outline of the poet's credentials. Maecenas would have appreciated them well. Instead the speaker plunges into the differences that shape their two existences so that the poem can exist as a looking glass for its recipient, to show him his own situation, posit a comparison between speaker and addressee, and, however subtly, suggest that Maecenas exchange his lot for Horace's and offer reasons why such an option is both meaningful and proper.

Horace twice uses the participle *sollicitus,* "troubled," in connection with his patron. The first, occurring in a general statement, looks to someone whose "troubled brow" (*sollicitam frontem*) could be smoothed by replacing wealth with poverty, elaborate with simple, urban affairs with country living, Rome with a Sabine valley.[55] The second is quite specific: Maecenas is *sollicitus* because he worries about the state, what befits it and what portends difficulty for it.[56] Both aspects of worry combine to portray Maecenas as rich (in Rome) and concerned about Rome, a double helping of cares that a visit to Horace away from the city, with all that such a movement implies, will cure. In between we have two stanzas that establish us in a temporal setting and proffer ways in which nature and man are analogical. It is the height of summer, a time when the shepherd seeks shade and water for his flock, warding off the sky's elemental heat. Among its celestial causes, along with Cepheus and the "star of the mad Lion" Horace lists Procyon, the chief star of Canis Minor and therefore close astronomical kin of Sirius-Canicula, the most prominent star in Canis Major and the brightest in the heavens. He thus draws us for a final time into the sequestered retreats of *c.* 1. 17 and 3. 13, the one offering a carefree setting for lyric song, the other a tangible source that is also inspiriting for the imagination.

What such an appearance in *c.* 3. 29 intimates is that the realm of water and shade is for Horace both literal and figurative at once. It is the landscape of the Sabine retreat, but it is also the mind of the poet and his refreshing, ennobling, instructive poetry. If we pursue Horace's meaning, Maecenas should be like the *pastor* (21) who has the instinct and intelligence to guide himself and his charges during a time of threat. He is the "shepherd" of Rome, attending to the people who are his charges and committed to their safety. (Horace, we must not forget, is also one of his "flock," as the recipient of the farm itself.) But in a still more abstract sense, Horace, too, is a shepherd, this time of Maecenas who here, now metaphysically, is the poet's worry. The only way that his patron can find peace of mind, the poet would seem to say, is by accepting an invitation to visit Horace, which is to say to enter his thoughts by listening to his words and falling under their spell.

As in *c.* 3. 4, the first half of the poem establishes the setting. Maecenas is to leave the city and commit himself to Horace's symposiastic festivity in a landscape that supports those who attend to its rich poetic essence. The second half offers a sustained, beautifully crafted meditation on one theme of that poetry for Maecenas' contemplation. Maecenas, the poem's initial stanzas urge, should make a crucial, one-time change in his life that may have positive repercussions for him. By the time we reach the ode's end, however, we have tracked a meditation on what the abstract fact of alternation itself means in life and on how we can best cope with the idea of mutability that most humans must regularly confront in their daily lives. Horace offers us three examples. Our momentary lot can be like a stream, now calmly flowing into the sea, now in spate raging destructively. Or we can be at the mercy of Jupiter who can bring a dark day or clear sky. Or there is Fortune, fickle goddess who, happy as she attends to her fierce business, is appropriately rendered in oxymoronic terms. Her task is to effect change in honors that are themselves insecure. She is kind now to the speaker, now to someone else.

At the start of the disquisition we are told in general terms that the person who is *aequus,* balanced and judicious in temper, while responding to life's foibles, will best be able to face the fluctuations of existence. He who has true self-knowledge and thus the inner security that comes from being at ease with one's psyche, Horace would seem to say, copes most easily in his spirit with whatever might come his way externally, whether positive or negative. He knows instinctively that the pendulum regularly swings now one way, now another, and that a mind at peace with itself remains unfazed by any form of mutability. Only at the end of the paradigm do we turn to the speaking "I" himself (53–56):

> laudo manentem: si celeris quatit
> pinnas, resigno quae dedit et mea
>   virtute me involvo probamque
>   pauperiem sine dote quaero.

> I praise [Fortune] while she stays. If she shakes her swift wings, I relinquish what she gave and I wrap myself in my virtue and I court upright poverty without a dowry.

Riches are not for him lest he have to pray to the gods to save his goods from the greedy sea. No literal merchantman will cause him concern lest it founder (62–64):

> tunc me biremis praesidio scaphae
> > tutum per Aegaeos tumultus
> > > aura feret geminusque Pollux.

> Then the breeze and twin Pollux will waft me safely
> through the Aegean's turmoils under the protection
> of a two-oared skiff.

The palpable boat that is laden with care-bringing possessions becomes the tiny symbolic rowboat of the innocent poet, married to the abstraction Poverty (*Pauperies*) if need be. The powerful change from literal to figurative grants us a final variation on the sacrosanctity theme that also takes us into the mind of the poet, which is as given to balance as it is untouchable by the physicality of the outer world.

But there is one word that stands out in these lines because of its allusivity back into the first poem of the collection, namely, *praesidio*. Horace means to alert his reader to his use of *praesidium* in apostrophe to characterize Maecenas in the second line of the initial poem of the collection:[57]

> o et praesidium et dulce decus meum . . .

> o both my bastion and my sweet grace.

The chiasmus the two poems create is thus both expansive and particular. The first ode of the collection and its penultimate masterpiece are each addressed to the poet's patron so that Maecenas himself and the way the poet sees their relationship become important elements of structure for the collection as a whole, and the repetition of *praesidium/praesidio* and of *meum*, attached to the neighboring *decus* but associated with *praesidium* as well, suggests an interchangeable possessiveness between poet and patron. Maecenas presents himself as bulwark, sheltering Horace from the pressures of reality, and the poet accepts and pinpoints the association. For all appearances the relationship is one of dependency: Horace will strike his head against the stars if his "bastion" ranks him among lyric bards. By the time we reach the conclusion of the penultimate ode, Horace has co-opted Maecenas' word for himself. All the protection he needs is a small skiff. His own inner security, and the imagination that projects it, is now assured by himself, not by any other. It is up to Maecenas to accept the poet's invitation and come away from Rome's difficulties and enter the poet's own literal world, which is also the figurative realm of thought and expression. The patron is beholden to the poet not only for the privilege of entering the latter's imagination but for the instruction, and the immortalizing, that results from his acceptance by poet into his poetry.

The skewing that the dedication of the first and the penultimate poems to Maecenas gives to the framing of the collection puts enormous stress on the final poem of the gathering, which begins with the famous claim "I have finished a monument more lasting than bronze" (*Exegi monumentum aere perennius*).[58] Balance in the outlining structure of the poetry books is to a degree righted by Horace's choice of the same meter, first asclepiadean, for initial and concluding odes, a meter used only in these two instances in the first three books of lyrics. But even this deliberate counterposition further reminds us that Maecenas is given the next-to-last and not the final ode. Unlike *c.* 2. 20, which concludes the second book of odes, *c.* 3. 30 shows the patron neither addressed nor mentioned. Neither is the emperor. In fact, the poem is a rarity in Horace for not using apostrophe or making use of the second person (three of the "Roman" odes fall into this category, and only a few other poems). Rarer still is the predominance of the speaking "I," which is instanced only once or twice elsewhere in the *Carmina*.

We find the first person particularly salient in *c*. 2. 20, an ode that has much in common with *c*. 3. 30. Both deal with the poet's immortality. In *c*. 2. 20 the *ego* turns into a swan, teaches barbarian tribes to become learned by knowledge of him, and needs no funeral rites or burial because of his presumed immortality. But the poem, for all its forthright individuality, is still addressed to Maecenas, and the word *vocas*, at line 6, reminds us of the human relationship between poet and patron, which immortal, cygneous Horace is now literally and figuratively above and beyond.

But there are other differences between *c*. 2. 20 and 3. 30 that establish the originality of the latter and help us find a context for it in Horace's private sphere of poetry that we have been searching out. The poem is a *monumentum* about a *monumentum*, a lapidary performance that, as critics have pointed out, smacks of an epitaph.[59] Horace is inscribing the "history" of his own eternal, poetic performance as envoi to his masterful collection. The gestures are grand, the boast expansive. His work will survive as long as priest and vestal climb the Capitolium. It will be read where he was born, humble but now the chief person to have acclimatized Greek lyric to Roman writing who can command Melpomene to crown him with Apollo's laurel. This would seem on the surface to be a very public poem, taking us from pyramids to Rome's most numinous hill, to Apulia, and, finally, to Greece and its muse. But comparison with the pyramids sets up a new version of sacrosanctity, with the poet's achievement now equivalent to the priest's, with each untouched by the ravages of time. Priest and vestal climbing the Capitoline may be an analogy for the continuity of poetry, as it claims a parallel with the continuity of religion, but it also verges on a metaphor for poetry itself, at least for the lyrics of Horace where ritual and art are often complementary.[60] His poetry is, of course, often concerned with religion in varying guises, but in a larger sense his art is also a type of rite, the performance of *carmina* in such a way as to move at least the sensibilities of its readers.

Finally we have the language of power. The speaker who directs the actions of the muse, in the poem's final lines, is also *princeps*, first among poets but also equivalent to none other than the prince of men, Augustus. He can draw Greek song to Italian measures, but the word I have blandly translated "draw," *deduxisse*, can also mean to "lead in triumph," as victor puts on display his vanquished subjects.[61] Horace's speaker not only behaves in a majestic manner, he culls the lexicon of political vocabulary to describe the force of his own accomplishment. But in fact, however public the appearance here of the vocabulary of tangible memorabilia, of religion, or of civic rule, it is used here to symbolize or, metaphorically, to distinguish poetry and poet and in fact to show the superiority of his imagination's performance over any palpable manifestations of authority, be they by priest or prince, *pontifex* or *princeps*. Their language is at the service of poetry and poet, not the other way around, in the valedictory that stamps the extraordinary grouping as a whole.

To conclude this preliminary survey let us turn to the emperor himself. In the first three books of the *Odes* Horace makes it clear that it remains in his competence to praise, and therefore to immortalize, Augustus but that such implicit allegiance is a matter of some delicacy and subject to a series of provisos. In a moment of Pindaric energy (*c.* 1. 12), Horace's speaker can verge on equating the emperor with gods and demigods, and Bacchic enthusiasm offers him the excuse to envision a future stellification of Augustus and incorporation into the *consilium Iovis* (*c.* 3. 25). But mostly the poet places us, and the emperor, in a situation defined by conditionality. In the ode preceding his yielding to Bacchus' inspiration, and to imagining the emperor's apotheosis, Horace alludes to an anonymous potentate who, should he wish to have "father of cities" (*pater urbium*)[62] inscribed among the *tituli* of his honorific statues, would not only have to do away with the madness of fratricidal war (*inpias caedis et rabiem . . . civicam*)[63] but to rein in license, eliminate reasons for ethical blame, and renew the *mores* of the people. In other words, our unnamed sovereign must not only end civil strife but restore traditional values. Only then, the juxtaposition of the two odes implies, will Bacchus encourage the poet to an act of immortalization.[64]

This conditionality is most intensely felt in the "Roman" odes that initiate book 3. We have seen how Horace, in the splendid fourth ode, makes much of establishing his credentials before advising the emperor, by the subterfuge of mythic exempla, on a military victor's proper behavior. The implication is that Augustus may, or may not, take his advice. The "results" of the poem lie in the future. Futurity takes a different form in the two poems that surround it. The third centers on the imperturbability of a person who is "just and tenacious of purpose." No tyrant, no thundering Jupiter, no disturbance of nature will shake his resolve:

> hac arte Pollux et vagus Hercules
> enisus arcis attigit igneas,
>   quos inter Augustus recumbens
>   purpureo bibet ore nectar, . . .[65]

> By this virtue Pollux and wandering Hercules in his struggle touched the fiery citadels, among whom reclining Augustus will drink nectar with ruddy lips

Augustus will join the company of gods (Bacchus, Pollux), demigods (Hercules) and deified Romulus (Quirinus), the presumption is, if, and only if, he remains not only honest but true to his purpose. This was the way toward immortality for Rome's founder. Such will it be for her renewer as well. The same notion is varied in the opening lines of the fifth ode:

> Caelo tonantem credidimus Iovem
> regnare: praesens divus habebitur
> Augustus adiectis Britannis
>   imperio gravibusque Persis.

> We have believed that thundering Jupiter reigns in heaven: Augustus will be considered a god among us when the Britons and the troublesome Parthians are added to the empire.

Augustus has yet to prove to the full his virtuosity as a hero, especially when dealing with foreign enemies, which now must be his vocation. Once the positive evidence is in, and his courage unchallenged, then the imminence of his godhead will be justified.

In both poems, and in fact generally throughout the first collection of lyrics, the divinity of Augustus is imagined as a possibility, but in the future. The poet in the present suggests ways for the emperor to attain such stature but leaves the results contingent. Only by taking to heart the poet's words will Augustus become worthy of immortality, an immortality which those very words are more likely to bestow than any other means.

In summary, Horace's treatment of Augustus complements the more general attitude he adopts in the first collection of *Carmina* of restraint when dealing with public affairs. He will preserve his privacy as vatic bard and eulogize Augustus in the present only when the emperor deserves such recognition. He will commit himself publicly to Rome when he is convinced that the state, too, is worthy of the permanent endorsement his genius alone can bestow. The final stanza of the sixth, and last, "Roman" ode intimates that such a time might be long distant:

> damnosa quid non inminuit dies?
> aetas parentum peior avis tulit
>   nos nequiores, mox daturos
>   progeniem vitiosiorem.[66]

> What has the destruction of time not diminished? The age of our parents, worse than that of our grandparents, has produced us still more wicked, soon about to engender a yet more degenerate progeny.

The cumulative vision in the first three books of odes that Horace creates of his private world, in which physical and spiritual, tangible and imagined, complement and reinforce each other, is a potent one. The poetry inspiring this portrait projects a speaker whose inner life battens on a self-confidence capable of exploiting country seclusion as a setting from which to offer commentary on the matter and manner of Rome's civic existence. There is little eulogistic in this appraisal and much that reserves judgment about the possibilities of future moral excellence, given the ambiguities of the city's ethical present and the potential for those in authority to wreak harm as well as good from their newly secured omnipotence.

The poetry is at their service for contemplation, and it has much to expound to the sage appreciator. The brilliance of the Bandusian fountain—or the shining surface of the tableware at a symposium—may make manifest to the writer, or to his fellow convivialists, the truth of themselves to themselves. This realization in turn, for the poet at least, may engender verse as honest and moving for its self-appraisal and for its insights into others, both as individuals and as parts of a community, as it is imaginative in presentation. It is the resultant poetry itself that can, and should, serve as a mirror for those in power if they are shrewd enough to seize the opportunity and to learn from it. But the creator of that poetry perseveres, throughout the collection, in dispensing his wisdom from a literal and figurative distance that on many levels separates him from those who might benefit from the message of his words.

When and for what reason, or reasons, Horace in his thinking abandoned this sequestered world overtly to endorse Rome, as city and symbol, and Augustus, its prince, can only be a matter for speculation. All we know is that such willing openness had become part of his thinking by the year 17 B.C.E., six years after the publication of the first lyric collection. For in that year the emperor decided to celebrate the *Ludi Saeculares* after an interval of a century and a third, and he chose Horace, and Horace accepted the proposition, to be the author of the *Carmen* to be sung on both the Palatine and Capitoline hills at the conclusion of the games' central days of sacrifice and prayer.[67]

The date was an appropriate one. It was fourteen years after the battle of Actium and the presumed end of civil war. Augustus' power seemed assured. His moral legislation had finally been passed in the preceding year (18 B.C.E.), allowing him to put his formal stamp on Rome's ethical patterning. The year of the *Ludi* also saw his adoption of Gaius and Lucius, the young sons of his daughter Julia and Agrippa.[68] The gesture is at once literal and symbolic. It affirms the continuity of the royal family, yet it also connotes Augustus' particular interest in youth and its importance for Rome's future, an interest that would find itself reified a few years later on the Ara Pacis Augustae. Both points—the need for strong ethical values and the dependence of Rome on its young—will figure prominently in Horace's poem.

For Horace to accept such a commission is to turn the metaphor of *c*. 3. 30 into reality: Horace will now literally share in a major moment of the state religion and become a type of priest, not accompanied by a vestal but training a choir of twenty-seven virginal boys and a like number of girls, all of noble families and all of whose parents were still alive, to sing his song as capstone and finale of the ritual celebration. The result was a crucial development in the poet's evolution, signifying both his public acceptance of Augustan Rome and his potential for affirming its stability.

Yet, as we would expect of such an autonomous genius as Horace, the resulting *Carmen,* however much it may seem to serve the communal purposes of the state and stand as highly visible evidence of the poet's allegiance to the city and its leader, nevertheless remains much the product of the poet's own individuality. For the ultimate power rests not with Augustan military, political, or even ethical prowess, however worthy of applause, but with the poet who in singing of them confirms their quality. It is he who, as creator of the event's finale, reconceives the proceedings in his imagination and who, in fact, puts his own individual stamp on them. It is also he alone who possesses the magic charm capable of bringing to fruition the prayers he utters through the chorus. Rome, its present and future, its immediate, tangible livelihood, and its ability to engage our attention more than two millennia after he wrote, is dependent on Horace's wit. However striking his accomplishment may be as inspiration for song, it is Augustus who is finally beholden to his poet, not vice versa.

Horace's poem must be placed in context. It is the climax of a long tradition of public performances of *carmina,* at least one of which had taken place at an earlier manifestation of the *Ludi.* It also draws on a rich literary heritage, both Greek and Roman. But first I will turn to the poem itself.

3

The *Carmen Saeculare*

The poem begins with the gods to be celebrated (1–8):[1]

> Phoebe silvarumque potens Diana,
> lucidum caeli decus, o colendi
> semper et culti, date quae precamur
>   tempore sacro,
>
> quo Sibyllini monuere versus
> virgines lectas puerosque castos
> dis, quibus septem placuere colles,
>   dicere carmen.

Phoebus and Diana, mistress of forests, brilliant grace of the heavens, O [you] worshipped and to be worshipped always, grant what we pray for at this holy time when the Sibyl's verses have advised that chosen maidens and chaste youths sing a hymn for the gods to whom the seven hills have given pleasure.

Horace's chorus begins by apostrophizing Apollo and Diana, recipients of the hymn just as they are patron divinities of the larger celebration. The particular names the poet chooses for them here, Phoebus and Diana, frame the song's initial line while their iteration also serves to structure the poem as a whole. As the ode draws to a conclusion we revert first to Phoebus (Apollo), as focus of lines 61 to 68, then to Diana, from 69 to 72, and in the poem's penultimate line both names are once more repeated. The imaginative satisfaction such wholeness of composition supplies, whether absorbed by hearing or by reading, complements the theme of recurrences and renewals that is basic to the poem's ideology. The cycle of the poem, brought before us most directly by divine nomenclature, is the aesthetic representation of the cycle of Rome's restoration, which the poem exemplifies, confirms, and brings into being.

The names Horace uses for the two divinities are also chosen for a specific purpose. Their root meanings, *phos-* in the case of Phoebus, *di-* for his sister, both endorse the brightness that accrues to them from their association, respectively, with the sun and the moon. This celestial radiance is confirmed in the appositional *lucidum caeli decus,* which merges the separate divinities into one brilliance that graces the heavens,[2] and then throughout the poem. We find it not only in the word *dies* itself (9, and reiterated punningly at 23 in the phrase *die claro*) but in the Sun's glistening chariot (*curru nitido,* 9), in Apollo's coruscating bow (*fulgente arcu,* 61), and in Diana's other names of Lucina (15) and Luna (36), the bringer for each individual human of light at birth and the continuous presence of luminosity in the night sky.

In calling attention at the start of his hymn to the clarity of the two gods in their astronomical manifestations, Horace is pointing up one of the major distinctions between Augustus' celebration of the *Ludi* and what we know of previous performances. We learn from Varro, as quoted by Censorinus, about the first certain observance of the *Ludi,* which occurred in 249 B.C.E. during the First Punic War. With the people frightened by prodigies, the *Decemviri sacris faciundis* consulted the Sibylline books, which ordered that games be proclaimed and appropriately dark victims be sacrificed to Dis Pater and Proserpina over a period of three nights. (We have no specifics about the next celebration in 149, or 146, but there is no reason to believe that the ritual was altered.)

Augustus changed this inheritance in two details of importance for the opening of the *Carmen*. First, daytime was as necessary as nighttime in the emperor's celebration, and certainly in Horace's lyric version day and its brightness take precedence over night, which is mentioned only once (24).[3] A second major divergence on Augustus' part from inherited tradition is the replacement of Hades and Proserpina, first by the Moerae during the initial proceedings at the Tarentum, then by Apollo and Diana as focal divinities for the final triduum. The nether regions and their implications of darkness and death are supplanted in Horace's initiating verses by the two most splendid heavenly bodies whose visibility is crucial for the orderly prosecution of our daily, monthly, and annual lives. The literal progress of the ceremony complements this alteration as we move from low ground and a setting where chthonic powers were worshipped to the heights of the Palatine and Capitoline with their implicit proximity to the divine sphere and its celestial manifestations.

In one further small but significant detail Horace's prayer differs from the oracle of the Sibyl, as quoted by Zosimus, outlining the *Ludi* to come. The priestess, according to the historian, asks that in the course of the ceremony somber-colored victims be sacrificed to the Moerae and that a black sow be offered to Earth.[4] The Parcae and Tellus do indeed receive stanzas that are adjacent in Horace's hymn, but in neither instance is darkness a part of the poet's design.

Besides brightness, Horace adds two other characteristics to Apollo and Diana in these opening lines, namely, might and glory. We will watch the particularities of divine power — in this instance of Diana's dominion over the natural world — unfold in the course of the poem. Here I would like to pause on the word *decus* and its implications both in this work and elsewhere in Horace. It appears, as we saw earlier, in the initial poem of Horace's first book of lyrics, directed to his patron Maecenas, also in the second line:

o et praesidium et dulce decus meum . . .

O both my bastion and my sweet grace.

Maecenas' role in the poet's life also is sustained by both authority and honor. He embodies the forcefulness to ward off unwanted intrusions into the poet's spiritual life and possesses the geniality to appreciate and adorn that life. For the *Carmen Saeculare*, as the private world of Horace's creative endeavors and its dependencies yield to the public sphere of Roman grandeur, we change from a human addressee and his sponsorship of Horace's imagination to two omnipotent gods who are asked to continue as advocates for Roman prosperity. The leap from one apostrophe to the other tells something of the poet's own development as he openly embraces the national enterprise of Rome.

The difference Horace thus adumbrates between his present and former selves is recapitulated when we turn to an even more salient topic of the opening stanza: time. The contrast of human with divine temporality is felt in the distinction between "we," the chorus of youths now hymning their prayer, and the gods who are the object of their invocation. But the presence of temporality is also felt in two other ways. First, it is used to reconfirm the immortality of Apollo and Diana. According to the chorus' apostrophe, the gods have always been, and will always be, worshipped (*o colendi / semper et culti*). As he moves us from past to future, the poet preserves the same verb, *colo*, as if to say that though mortal time mutates from what has happened to what will, the gods remain the same, as steady, constant, and finally atemporal as the heavenly elements who share in their being.

Meanwhile divine and human temporalities merge in a second aspect of time: the specific, sacred moment of festival celebration. Horace underscores the conjunction figuratively by the assonantal connection between *semper* and *tempore*. If the juxtaposition of *colendi* and *culti* represents the sempiternity of the gods and their human worship, the sonic echo of *semper* in *tempore* suggests aurally that, at this incantatory moment when the chorus chants its hymn of supplication, the poet's Orphic power brings the two spheres together. For at least the instant of song's duration, the immediacies of human time, the date of June 3, 17 B.C.E., as well as the age of the choristers positioned as virginal youth still to face the multivalent challenges of adulthood, blend with the divine sphere while at the same time reminding the twin gods of their duty responsibly to oversee human affairs.[5]

We should also look beyond the necessary chastity of the performers to the more general significance of youth in Augustan ideology. It is particularly appropriate here that singers at an early stage of life be the protagonists in bringing into being the fresh *saeculum*, eliciting the new from the old, paralleling past ceremony while both renewing and innovating.

For the first of several times Horace also co-opts other voices into his singular utterance. Here it is the verses of the Sibyl whose admonition forced the poet's inspiration into being and whose authority supplements the words voiced by the chorus. *Monuere* likewise participates in both past and future. In this instance the Sibyl reminds Rome and its rulers of their duty to adhere to a tradition from the past that must be repeated in the future, and such remembrance, conveyed to her devotees in the stichic precision of hexameter verse, became one of several causes behind Horace's own lyric masterpiece. Presumably to forget the regularity of prayer, especially of prayer projected on the grand scale of the *Ludi Saeculares,* is to incur the possibility of divine displeasure.

These stanzas are also typical of the poem as a whole in foregrounding stylistic figures associated with beauty of sound, such as alliteration and assonance. This is only natural in a poem that must have conveyed much of its initial impact from the way its listeners heard it. Here, for instance, we notice how "d" sounds, in particular "-di," run through these quatrains, linking Apollo and Diana to the grace that is theirs (*decus*), to their continuous worship (*colendi*), and to the prayer offered to them (*date*). These topics take us in turn to the gods (*dis*), to the song they will receive (*dicere*), and to the day (*diem*) of its presentation, which opens the next stanza. Time and again throughout the poem it is the efficacy of the verses as sung that helps give the poem its special power. This is as true now, when the educated reader must reperform the ode orally to attempt to garner its full potential, as it would have been at its initial presentation.

If the first stanza makes the idea of space crucial by asking us to cast our eyes heavenward at the graceful orbs of sun and moon, the second locates us terrestrially, in the immediacy of Rome's seven hills. Their particularity will be of significance at a later, counterbalancing moment as the poem draws to an end, with a reminder, first, that it is after all in front of Apollo's "altars on the Palatine" (*Palatinas aras,* 65) that the celebration is taking place and, then, of the importance of the Aventine (69) for the worship of Diana. Here we must pause for a moment on the poet's use of the phrase *septem colles* to designate Rome's seven eminences. Horace is the first recorded author to use the word *colles* ("hills") in this context and a look at the usage of other contemporary or near-contemporary authors may help clarify his purpose here.

The first mention of the proverbial "seven hills" is found in Varro, writing in the years immediately preceding Cicero's death: "Where Rome now is was called the Septimontium from the same number of mountains which the city afterwards embraced within its walls."[6] Next chronologically comes Virgil, who in the *Georgics* speaks of the development of "most beautiful Rome":

> . . . septemque una sibi muro circumdedit arces.

> and who uniquely enclosed her seven citadels with a wall.[7]

We then have Tibullus who speaks of Rome's *septem montibus* and Propertius referring to its *septem iugis* (seven ridges), both elegists at work contemporaneously with the writing of the *Aeneid*.[8] Our last Augustan witness, Ovid, some two decades later, in the *Fasti*, uses the mouthpiece of Carmentis, mother of Evander, to predict the future:

> "fallor, an hi fient ingentia moenia colles, . . . ?"

> "Am I deceived, or will these hills become massive walls?"[9]

The theme that runs through the majority of these references is the association of Rome's topographical heights with walls and hence with the need for martial fortifications.[10] The hills are enclosed by bulwarks in Varro's definition. Virgil expands the point poetically by turning the heights metaphorically into citadels, and, finally, Ovid resorts to metamorphosis as the hills actually become the city's defensive ramparts. In this intellectual continuum, only the references in Tibullus and Propertius are what we might style neutral, and even Propertius' mention of *iuga* in this context carries secondary connotations of bondage imposed by, or on, the city.

Horace's initiating use of *colles*, therefore, not only moderates the imposing eminences that the word *montes* suggests but deliberately lacks the militaristic implications that the "hills" receive in Varro and Virgil and which they actually are made by mutation to adopt at Ovid's hands. His lexical choice sets a tone for the ode as it evolves whereby Rome's bellicose propensities and cravings for vengeance are suppressed, or deflected, in favor of the workings of moderation and the peaceful applications of power.

Direct mention of the Palatine is saved for the poem's conclusion, but already in the second stanza we have an oblique reminder of the ceremony's location.[11] We can presume from references in the sixth book of Virgil's *Aeneid* and in Tibullus' most elaborate elegy, 2. 5, that the Sibylline books had been placed in the Temple of Palatine Apollo probably as early as 28 B.C.E. and certainly by 18, a year before the *Ludi* took place.[12] The initial audience of Horace's poem, standing before Apollo's white marble shrine, would easily have thought of the Sibyl's hexameter pronouncements, stored within.

There is less indirection about allusion to the Palatine in the poem's third stanza (9–12):

> alme sol, curru nitido diem qui
> promis et celas aliusque et idem
> nasceris, possis nihil urbe Roma
>   visere maius.

> O nourishing Sun, who on your gleaming chariot bring forth the day and hide it, and are reborn another and the same, may you be able to behold nothing greater than the city of Rome.

As Horace focuses on Phoebus Apollo's role as sun god, he asks us to imagine our inner eye operating in two directions. First is our view of the sun as we behold it in the heavens and contemplate the paradox of change and stability, alternation and sameness, that it incorporates along with its constancy of nourishment. But we are also expected to accept the posture of the sun god himself looking down from above on Rome and on the seven hills that define it and, according to the poet's prayer, conceiving no greater vision in his purview than the city itself. We are asked to contemplate Apollo contemplating Rome, and us, and blessing the city's *maiestas*.[13]

There is a more immediate vertical vision also at work here that several critics have suggested.[14] Again it involves views from above and from below but nearer to hand. Horace claims our attention once again for the Temple of Palatine Apollo but now with a particular focus on its pediment. There "on the gable's peak" (*supra fastigia*), as Propertius tells us in an elegy written some ten years before our celebration, stood a replication of the chariot of the Sun (*Solis currus*), Apollo now reified as the Sun looming over the front of his temple.[15] The crest of the temple, the terrestrial surrogate for heaven's loftiness, would be the highest point on the Palatine whence the god's sculptured appearance would look down on the crowd who share in the proceedings as the chorus raises its hymn upwards toward him in prayer.

This moment would be logical for Horace to make some mention of what Propertius next tells us in his elegy and what the admiring eye would in fact see as it traveled down from the gable, with its gleaming sculpture, to the altar in front of the temple. This new sight would be the temple's twin doors, which contained replications in ivory of two acts of retribution on Apollo's part, against Brennus and his fellow Gauls for attacking his shrine at Delphi and against Niobe for her boastfulness toward Leto and her twin offspring, acts whose representations were the initial focus of attention of those privileged to enter the temple proper.[16] But Horace here forfeits any mention of these scenes, nor does he seize the occasion to allude to the adjacent portico of the Danaids and to the statues of the father and his throng of daughters who presumably are to be interpreted here as preparing to butcher their husbands on their wedding night.[17] In both groups of sculpture, adorning doors or portico, the notion of vendetta leading to death is paramount.

However prominent in Augustan iconology elsewhere, none of this negative tonality enters the *Carmen Saeculare*. Rather we find in the address to Sol other, positive themes that permeate the poem. The first is the sun's fostering presence (*alme*) and its implications of growth and fertility. Horace calls attention to the epithet by anomaly. With one rule-proving exception in Plautus where Hercules is entitled "my nourishing nurse,"[18] this is the first instance in Latin where *almus* is applied to a male divinity. Since the adjective is regularly associated not only with goddesses but with *dies* and *lux*,[19] Horace associates Apollo with both male and female principles, being born and yet producing the new day, nourished and nourisher at once.

The second theme the stanza renews is that of the luminosity of the ever-present, ever-mutating celestial body, which the poet playfully recreates for us by the anagrammatic relation he develops between *diem* and *idem*. The bright day that the sun brings is, like the orb itself, always the same and always different, renewed and renewing. Furthermore, the sun is both immortal, all-seeing, and capable, as it were, of apprehending not only Rome the city, but the breadth of its empire. Yet it is also, like that city and empire, ever changing and evolving as well in its history over time. Finally, the stress on both is complemented by the dichotomy of concealment and exposure. We are after all bearing witness along with the gods themselves to the birth and rebirth of Rome.[20] This renewal Apollo as the god of the sun both sustains and mirrors in his own daily progress.[21]

The theme of birth and promulgation continues in the forefront of the next stanzas as we turn from Apollo to his sister (13–24):

> Rite maturos aperire partus
> lenis, Ilithyia, tuere matres,
> sive tu Lucina probas vocari
>   seu Genitalis:
>
> diva, producas subolem patrumque
> prosperes decreta super iugandis
> feminis prolisque novae feraci
>   lege marita,
>
> certus undenos deciens per annos
> orbis ut cantus referatque ludos
> ter die claro totiensque grata
>   nocte frequentis.

> Ilithyia, gracious at fittingly bringing forth offspring in due season, protect our mothers, whether you wish to be called Lucina or Genitalis: goddess, rear our youth and bless the decrees of the fathers concerned with women and their need for wedlock and on the marriage-law, fruitful of new progeny, so that the sure cycle of ten times eleven years may bring back singing and games thronged three times in day's brilliance and as often during the welcome of night.

Following the *tu*-form familiar from hymnic tradition, Horace addresses Diana with three names fitting for her role as goddess of birth. All bring particular force to their context. Although the Ilithyiae figure both in the inscription of the *Acta* and in the Sibylline oracle, this is the first instance of such a designation for Diana in Latin literature.[22] It brings with it affiliations with the beginnings of Greek literature from Homer on, in particular with the Homeric Hymn to Apollo, while the goddess' epithet Lucina not only has associations with childbirth in Latin literature as early as Plautus but is particularly suitable in a context that foregrounds the presence of light and its conjunction with life. Finally there is the appelative *Genitalis*, which Horace, here, apparently invents as attribute for Diana the Light-Bringer. The title reconfirms both the connection of Diana with birth and the continued importance of generation, and regeneration, at the initiation of Horace's poem.

Horace appropriately places the stress here on mothers and motherhood. He strengthens the link of Diana with maternity by two figurative chains based on assonance and alliteration. The first is the reverberation of the *-tu* sound that takes us from *maturos . . . partus* to *tuere* to the hymnic *tu*, where the resonance links the addressee first with fortunate birth, then with the protection of those born. Instead of repeating the word "you" while varying the goddess's epithets, as in the standard procedure of hymn, Horace absorbs the potency of such a litany into the very words that assure her creative imminence in human affairs.[23] The second chain takes us from *maturos* and *partus* to *matres*, carefully linking through sound the mothers with the offspring they will bear with Diana's timely help.

The next stanza, with its ironic bounding by *diva* and *marita*, virgin goddess and laws sustaining marriage, furthers the association of women with Diana, but now the *matres* are suitably conjoined to *patres* (the word *patrumque*, ending line 17, recalls in sound *partus*, which concludes the initial line of the preceding stanza).[24] It is only through the "marriage," as it were, of the two through the union of bountiful mothers and supportive fathers, the city senators, that the child that is Rome can remain in existence or, better in this setting, come now into reinvigo-rated being.²⁵ The stanza itself offers a miniature example of lexical fruitfulness, of poetry's generative capability that mim-ics the fertility for which the verses pray. The juxtaposition of *producas* and *subolem,* the "producing" and the reality of "off-spring," brings forth, lexically, the "progeny" who are the object of concern since *proles* derives from *pro* plus the same root from which *suboles* evolves.²⁶

This act of poetic generation, supporting and mimicking lin-guistically the human creativity of which it tells, is underscored within the stanza by other means. Not least is the personifica-tion, which here means the humanizing, of the law in question, which is itself said to be "wedded" and "fruitful" (*feraci*) of new issue. Ordinarily in Latin, from Plautus on, *maritus* means "having a husband or wife, married." Since *lex* is an abstract noun, Horace coins a new sense for the adjective as "relating to marriage, conjugal, nuptial." But poetry allows both purports to signify. For the poet, a law about marriage becomes personi-fied and is, appropriately, both "married" and "fertile," capable of begetting like a living organism. Again the magic of poetry turns abstract into concrete, animates the inanimate and, as it were, during the course of the stanza gives the *decreta patrum* the human dimension they were meant to achieve. The evolution of language once more echoes the production of which it tells.

The word *prolis,* as the last of five words spread over ten lines beginning with the prefix *pro-,* likewise plays a vital role in this literal and figurative process of begetting. It takes us back not only within its own stanza (*producas, prosperes*) but also to the two preceding quatrains (*promis, probas*) to form a lexical climax centered on what the dictionary defines, for *pro-,* as "the sense of forward movement or direction," "the . . . idea of bringing into the open." We begin with the sun's "bringing forth" the day, move on to Diana and her "approval" of the nomenclature of begetting, and reach a culmination here as the choristers ask the goddess to center the force of her goodwill on strengthening the lineage of Rome.

The root meaning of *ferax* continues on into the final stanza of the sentence through the compound *referat*. The result of this segment of the prayer is that Diana will not only foster the fertility of individual Romans but will "bring (about) again" the singing and the games that stand for the renewal itself. The Sibylline oracle at its start, we should remember, defines the hundred-and-ten year cycle as "the longest span of life for men."[27] Three aspects of time thus merge here: the generic time of human birth, the specific triduum devoted to the religious ceremonies of these specific *Ludi,* and the century-plus span of the presumably longest possible human life. Horace carefully interassociates the trio. There must be fertility to have celebrants, the ritual must take place in its set period, and the span between its recurrences must coincide with that of an extraordinary human existence. Rome itself, in this remarkable progress, is thus like a man's individual life expanded to the grandest scale. It, too, must needs suffer renewal after it has lived out its own due extent of time. Diana—and her *Ludi*—will implement this process of "secularity."

Just as *feraci* is picked up by *referat* as linguistic illustration of the co-optation of specific aspects of fertility by wider reaches of generative processes, so *decreta* is etymologically echoed in *certus.* The decrees of the fathers are complemented by promises from heaven of endurance. The *decreta* engender not children specifically but the reassurance that Rome will continue to mark its longevity by notching grand spans of mortal existence to mark its course, as particular lives defined by human *saecula* blend into, and themselves also define, the larger sweep of historical time.

But other divine help is also necessary (25–28):

Vosque, veraces cecinisse Parcae,
quod semel dictum est stabilisque rerum
terminus servet, bona iam peractis
      iungite fata.

And you, Fates, truthful in your song, as was once
ordained and may the steady hand of events confirm
it, join happy destinies to those now past.

One song anticipates another. Once more Horace's charming
verbal music is confirmed by, while at the same time absorbing and reprojecting the potency of, another powerful song, and
the singing during the ceremony (*cantus*), with its specific goals,
is corroborated by the grander efficacy of the Fates' chanting
(*cecinisse*) and its truth-telling.[28] Likewise, the utterance of the
Fates shares with the worship of Apollo and Diana the fact
that it looks to both past and future. Just as the twin gods have
been, and always will be, the subject of human adoration, so the
Fates look to what has happened while predicting good things
to come.

In this context the command *iungite* takes on pointed overtones. It is not long since the poet has used the phrase *iugan-
dis feminis* (18–19) to help distinguish the specific marriage laws
dictated by the senate fathers to assure Rome's continuity. The
prayer to the Fates looks to the grander stretches of time that
the previous stanza had suggested and asks for the still more
ambitious union of brilliant past with auspicious future. Horace
calls attention to the opening line of the quatrain in two ways.
First, he invents a new grammatical usage: this is the first exampled use of the adjective *verax* with the infinitive.[29] Second,
he pointedly adopts the Roman designation Parcae for the Fates
in place of the Greek Moerae, which appears in both the oracle,
as quoted by Zosimus (8), and the inscription of the *Acta* (64).

I will return later to the significance of Horace's word choice for purposes of literary allusion to Catullus and Virgil. But it is worth noting here how the context also sanctions Horace's use of the name "Parcae" as a salient example of *figura etymologica*. Aulus Gellius informs us that the learned Varro connected *Parca* with *pario*, "to bear offspring": "For *Parca* . . . is derived from *partus* with the change of one letter."[30] In reminding us that the Parcae, at least to the ancient reader, are lexically linked to the idea of parturition, Horace connects their song, and his, with all the images of gestation that have permeated the preceding verses. On this occasion, like the imposing song of the Fates, the birth itself is a particularly majestic one, namely, the fated ongoing renaissance of Rome itself.

And nature, too, is asked to share in this fecundity (29–32):

> fertilis frugum pecorisque Tellus
> spicea donet Cererem corona;
> nutriant fetus et aquae salubres
>   et Iovis aurae.

> May Earth, teeming with crops and cattle, offer
> Ceres a wreath of corn; may the healthful rains and
> breezes of Jupiter nourish the harvest.

Growth in inanimate nature must parallel and accompany, according to the hymn's prayer, the regeneration of humankind. Here, too, the stanza's figurative structure, which helps project these notions, is splendidly compact within itself. *Fertilis* anticipates both the immediate *frugum* and more distant *fetus* by alliteration while assonance binds it to *Tellus,* helping to form a verbal embrace for the flora and fauna that earth in its bounty will continue to nurture. Likewise alliteration links *aquae* and *aurae* while their attributes, *salubres* and *Iovis,* in their mutual interchangeability, both merge and distinguish the water and air essential for sustaining cultivation. *Fertilis,* through its etymology, likewise looks beyond the stanza to words like *ferax* (19) and *referat* (22). The fertility of the agricultural world is a crucial complement to the fruitfulness of human nature (and the laws that encourage it) as well as to the *Ludi* whose performance will reaffirm its potency with the aid not only of Leto's offspring but of goddesses who succor the earth and of the beneficent king of the immortals in his guise as celestial provider of the elements necessary for the survival of mankind.

Here again Varro offers us help not only in elucidating the structure of a stanza circumscribed by the divinities Tellus and Jupiter but in underscoring fertility as its major theme. As introduction to his *Res Rustica,* he invokes twelve gods who are particular patrons of husbandmen. Jupiter and Tellus head the list:[31]

> Primum, qui omnis fructus agri culturae caelo et terra continent, Iovem et Tellurem; itaque, quod ii parentes magni dicuntur, Iuppiter pater appellatur, Tellus Terra mater.

> First Jupiter and Tellus who, by means of the sky and the earth, control all the yield of agriculture; and so it is that, as they are said to be mighty parents, Jupiter is called Father, Tellus Mother Earth.

Varro's next set of divinities to be addressed by farmers helps connect Horace's verses here to the *Carmen* as a whole:

> Secundo Solem et Lunam quorum tempora observantur, cum quaedam seruntur et conduntur.

> In the second place Sun and Moon whose appearances are watched when crops are sowed and harvested.

Apollo and Diana, in their roles as divinities of sun and moon, have vital shares in the landsman's practical affairs, supporting the fecundity of his earth. (Horace stresses the connection by apostrophizing Diana as Luna in the subsequent stanza for the only occasion in the poem.) In Varro's third place we find Ceres, central to the poet's stanza as she is to the productivity that its prayer anticipates.[32]

Finally, as critics point out,[33] the literary combination of the divinities Tellus and Ceres, especially given their strong connections with earth and with Jupiter's water and air, finds its sculptural counterpart in the best preserved of the four grand reliefs adorning the Ara Pacis Augustae, whose construction was decreed four years after the *Ludi* were performed. The panel's central figure has been variously interpreted as Terra Mater, Italia, and Pax as well as Ceres and Tellus, and no doubt aspects of all five would be discerned by the ancient viewer. Horace's words give particular voice to art's intimations not only of earth's regenerative ability but of the health that accompanies the Augustan peace.

Then, in the stanza before the poem's pivotal quatrain, Horace returns whence he started (33–36):

> condito mitis placidusque telo
> supplices audi pueros, Apollo;
> siderum regina bicornis, audi,
>   Luna, puellas.

> Apollo, gentle and calm, with your weapon put away, hear the suppliant youths; Luna, crescent queen of the stars, hear the girls.

We follow circularly back, in standard ring-composition, to the ode's beginning with its preeminent addressees and its choristers, for purposes of review as well as for an initial rounding off. Horace has reached a point where summation is necessary, bringing to culmination and conclusion nine potent stanzas centered on god, goddess, and Fates and on their role in bringing about renewed fecundity. But there are notable differences between beginning and initial recapitulation. For the first time we are told that the male divinity should heed the boys, while the girls should be the object of Diana's attention, as if the act of performance as well as its results had now become a factor of significance in the ode's evolution.

Moreover, ambiguity shades the description of the apostrophe itself. In the opening stanza there is no doubt that "we," the chorus of boys and girls, are uttering the hymn of prayer. Now, with the suppression of any reference to the first person plural, we must still be listening to the youthful singers but we also sense the secondary resonance of the chorus leader, who happens to be the creator of the poem, in fact commanding the gods to listen to their petitioners. We have the first direct inkling of a notion that will become dominant in the poem's concluding stanzas: the power of Horace's song to accomplish in actuality that for which his mouthpieces are pleading.

But the most critical mutation is in the nomenclature and attributes of the gods themselves. From Phoebus and Diana/ Ilithyia/Lucina/Genitalis we turn to Apollo and Luna. Apollo is mild and peaceful, but the implication is that he has sequestered his destructive shafts, which, in a less benign mood, he could readily put to use. Perhaps he has even recently done so. Let us look at the several possibilities, all of which may be in some degree operative here.[34] Apollo could use his weaponry in his role as god who dispenses both diseases and their cures. In literature he appears first in the former position, carrying plague to the Greeks who have offended his priest.[35] As god of medicine, instead of harbinger of disease, his renewed presence in the poem would dovetail neatly with Jupiter's health-giving breezes mentioned in the previous stanza. In keeping with his positive tone throughout the *Carmen*, Horace merely hints at what could have been a major negative aspect of the god's power. Readers of Horace have seen it surface in *c.* 1. 21, his earliest ode concerned with both Apollo and Diana, a lyric where the speaker directs the performance of a hymn and in the end announces:

> hic bellum lacrimosum, hic miseram famem
> pestemque a populo et principe Caesare in
> > Persas atque Britannos
> > > vestra motus aget prece.

> Moved by your prayer, he [Apollo] will drive tearful war, will drive sad hunger and disease from the people and Caesar their prince onto the Persians and the Britons.

In the *Carmen Saeculare,* paean is replaced by brief pronouncement that the plague-bearing god has given way to Apollo Medicus who will now support his father's beneficial intentions.

Mention of Apollo's weapon (*telum*) also serves as a reminder of the god's interest in the hunt, and a reader of the recently published *Aeneid* would well remember how hunting also adumbrates death in the simile where Aeneas, about to set out with Dido on the chase that heralds her demise, is compared to quivered Apollo "on [whose] shoulders shafts clang."[36] The metaphoric wound that Aeneas the hunter has already inflicted on his prey will soon become the literal wound of her suicide, and Virgil's clear reminiscence of the opening of the *Iliad* is a further acknowledgment of the god's deathly power, which will now be suppressed just as his arrows remain unused in their quiver.

For those present before the Apollo temple, the reading of the *Carmen* would combine with recollections of the *Aeneid* to invoke another Apollo who will gain greater prominence as the poem progresses, one who presided over Augustus' victory at Actium:

Actius haec cernens arcum intendebat Apollo . . .

Beholding these things Apollo of Actium was stretching his bow.[37]

This Apollo has several names. Propertius calls him Navalis as well as Actius, again, and Ovid styles him Actiacus.[38] Because he was Augustus' patron divinity and the song is being performed before his temple, it is only apt that we ponder here also his role as god of war and, in particular, as crucial presence during the battle in which Augustus brought an end to civil war and validated his position as supreme ruler of Rome. Apollo's decisive bow and arrows can now be discarded as he brings his favor to the *Pax Augusta* and to Rome's refoundation based on moral strength at home and foreign peace grounded on martial firmness.

Perhaps also Diana/Luna's epithet *bicornis* in this context absorbs something of her brother's attributes. The word receives particular stress. This is its only appearance in Horace, and it is unique in Latin with this meaning. Although the attribute *silvarum potens* and mention of Mount Algidus as the poem draws to a close remind us of Diana's association with the wild, Horace makes no direct allusion in his hymn to Diana as goddess of the chase. But *bicornis* may offer some hint of a reference that his readers might expect in a *laudatio* of the goddess. The crescent moon is hornlike in its arch, curved at both ends like a hunter's bow. If we are meant to think for a moment of Diana as goddess of the hunt, and of how easily hunting shades into war, then, though less directly than in the case of Apollo, Horace deflects any violence implicit in Diana's mythology away from mankind by an act of stellification that mutates the real horn of her bow into the metaphorical "horns" of her burgeoning moon in heaven.[39]

At the center of the poem we return to Rome, but Rome now is not just the city with seven hills and the site of a glorious celebration but an entity with a historical past and with the presumption of a notable future. Rome, too, has its own beginnings and rebeginnings, and these now become the special focus of the poet's enterprise (37–48):

Roma si vestrum est opus Iliaeque
litus Etruscum tenuere turmae,
iussa pars mutare lares et urbem
    sospite cursu,

cui per ardentem sine fraude Troiam
castus Aeneas patriae superstes
liberum munivit iter, daturus
    plura relictis:

di, probos mores docili iuventae,
di, senectuti placidae quietem,
Romulae genti date remque prolemque
    et decus omne.

If Rome be your monument and if Ilian bands held the Etruscan shore, a remnant ordered to change their homes and city in a course that brings no harm, for whom chaste Aeneas, survivor of his fatherland, without harm through Troy's conflagration paved a way for freedom, about to bestow more [good] things than were left behind [at Troy]: gods, grant upright ways to our educable youth, gods, [grant] peace to [those in the] calm of old age, [grant] to the race of Romulus both resources and offspring and every distinction.

We have, in a lyric précis, the story of Aeneas, which is to say, the saga of Rome's inception. Her *opus*, the steadiness of her monumentality as created by the gods but reinvented as an intellectual exercise by Horace and his celebrants, begins with Troy and ends on the western shore of Italy.[40] It involves the exchange of a city destroyed for another still incipient, but, in Horace's telling, there is no diminution of power in the interchange. *Turmae* should not lose here the essential meaning which it has, for instance, in the *Aeneid*, of squadrons of cavalry,[41] and Aeneas' primary action is metaphorically the paving of a way for freedom, which is to say, according to the etymology of *munio*, its spiritual fortification.[42] The literal loss of a city is replaced by a figurative strength that at the start, and from then on, lay behind Rome's quest for *libertas*.[43]

But it is Aeneas who is at the core of these lines and in particular his trial by fire at the moment of Troy's collapse. The holiness that the adjective *sospes* attaches to the journey of freedom now becomes centered on the founder himself and his sacrosanctity.[44] But there is also a particular resonance here. The preeminent Roman festival that involved a trial by fire was the Parilia, held on the Palatine on April 21 to honor the birthday of the city.[45] Tibullus, in elegy 2. 5, describes the moment in its proceedings when a shepherd leaps through the flames in an act of purgation:

> ille [pastor] levis stipulae sollemnis potus acervos
>   accendet, flammas transilietque sacras.

> Drunk, the shepherd will ignite the heaps of light
> straw as prescribed, and will leap across the sacred
> flames.[46]

Ovid helps us be more specific about the connection with Aeneas. In his discussion in the *Fasti* of the origin of the Parilia and, in particular, of the etiology of its trial by fire, he offers several explanations. The most historically oriented involves Rome's founding hero at Troy:

> an magis hunc morem pietas Aeneia fecit,
> innocuum victo cui dedit ignis iter?

> or rather did the piety of Aeneas make this custom
> to whom, though conquered, the fire granted a road
> unscathed? [47]

Ovid is clearly thinking back to Horace's description here. The path of freedom is replaced by the path through fire. *Ardentem Troiam* is transformed into Ovid's *ignis* while the unharmed hero (*sine fraude*) becomes the fiery passage that brings him no hurt (*innocuum*).[48]

These parallels are for a purpose. Ovid has forthrightly expressed what Horace leaves indirect: the trial by fire is the earlier poet's way of associating Aeneas not only with the birth of Rome out of Troy but with the particularities of its celebration on April 21. As we start the second half of the poem we are still deeply involved with the world of birth and new beginnings. Now, however, we have been drawn into not so much the generic procreation of Rome and its inhabitants as specifically the historical establishment of the city by Aeneas and its heroic initiation through the moral refinement of Troy's fire.

Ovid makes one further change that draws our attention to an unexpected turn in Horace's description of Aeneas. For the later poet it is Aeneas' *pietas*, a characteristic Virgil had mapped so fully in the *Aeneid*, that is the hero's saving virtue in his time of testing. Horace's replacement of his wonted piety with the attribute *castus* serves several purposes. On a general level Aeneas is pure, that is, a worthy figure to serve as model for a religious ritual of consequence. More particularly, he is sexually chaste and therefore an appropriate prototype for Roman youth to emulate. The balanced connection with the *pueri casti* at the opening of the poem is clear. At the initiation rite of Rome's beginning, it is Aeneas' *castitas* that both preserved him and set a pattern for the future. In Horace's song, memorializing a ritual of Rome's rebirth, it is Aeneas' literal and spiritual descendants, the youth of Rome, who duly serve as the mouthpieces for the capstone of the *Ludi*'s proceedings. Just as the physical demise of Troy serves as platform for spiritual renovation and not for further bloodshed, so archetypal chastity remains an exemplar for its modern representation.[49]

Finally, Horace himself can serve as commentator on the stanza's meaning. In the third of the "Roman" odes, *c*. 3. 3, Juno indicts Troy for the immorality involved in its demise, caused by Paris, an "unchaste judge" (*incestus iudex*, 19) and a "foreign woman," namely Helen. Troy was (21–24):

> . . . ex quo destituit deos
> mercede pacta Laomedon, mihi
>   castaeque damnatum Minervae
>   cum populo et duce fraudulento.

> condemned to me and to chaste Minerva, along with its people and deceitful leader, ever since Laomedon cheated the gods of the agreed-upon award.

The parallel wording with lines 41–44 of the *Carmen* serves two purposes. It stresses the fact that the Aeneas who sets a pattern for moral uprightness at Rome's start will be unlike the adulterous, deceiving Paris and akin to chaste Minerva and exacting Juno. It also suggests that we read the phrase *sine fraude* in two ways. Holy, moral Aeneas penetrates Troy's fire without injury. He also makes his way from the burning city "without deceit," that is, untouched by its ancestral *fraus*, initiated by Laomedon and inherited by Priam. Virgil in the first book of the *Georgics* can speak of the "perjuries of Laomedon's Troy" for which "we" Romans are still paying the penalty.[50] Horace in the *Carmen* imagines away this corrupt and corrupting legacy and thereby purges both Rome's beginning and, appropriately, the city's present renewal fostered by Aeneas' alter ego. The new foundation and its leader will be a paragon both chaste and incapable of suffering harm.[51]

The participle *daturus* also reaches out into the poem in a way that complements and extends the poet's bow toward Aeneas. The verb is used only twice elsewhere in the *Carmen,* each time in the form of the imperative *date*. The first is in the ode's third line as the chorus initiates its prayer to Apollo and Diana. The second occurs in line 47 in a further double apostrophe, in anaphora, to the gods (*di*), immediately subsequent to the mention of Aeneas.[52] By conferring on Aeneas the same verb, *dare*, in the future that he twice associates with the gods in the commands of prayer, Horace linguistically links Rome's founding hero with the gods who, we may assume, here consist of the Olympic pantheon and not merely of Apollo and Diana. The repetition *date, daturus, date* brings implicit apotheosis to Aeneas as well.

The iteration of *dare* also links Aeneas with the next stanza and with the race of Romulus.[53] Mention of the first begetter leads easily to the next of Rome's founding fathers and to her actual namer. But it is reference to Rome's youth (*iuventa*) and its morality that helps form the most obvious transition from chaste Aeneas to his modern progeny. The singers pray to the gods for "offspring" (*prolis*) for Romulus' people just as earlier they had asked Diana to encourage the law that brought them into being (*prolis*, 19).[54] Likewise the request for *decus* serves as a reminder of the role of Apollo and Diana, *lucidum caeli decus,* in bringing about renewed quest for distinction. But it is the poet's dwelling on the need for upright morality for Rome's youth and quiet calm for its elders that distinguishes these verses from the ode's initial segments. Horace is now concerned not only with progeny per se but with their behavior and contentment, especially their peaceful and prosperous well-being (*rem*), as they pass through life from youth to age. As we enter the specifics of Rome's foundation and chronicle her history from Troy to the present, we must also be concerned with education and with the ethics of proper behavior that must be implemented if Rome is to remain worthy of her heritage.

Lines 45–48 are also noteworthy for the intense music of their sound, a characteristic, as we noted earlier, of the poem as a whole. Here, for example, we observe how initial "d" sounds interconnect gods (*di*, in anaphora) with teaching (*docili*), prayer (*date*) and grace (*decus*), while the concluding syllables "-li" or "-ti" conjoin teachable youth (*docili*), again, with their elders (*senectuti*) to form the race (*genti*) of Romulus. Then as now the reverberations would help the educated listener make the multitude of intellectual links that the poet's words intimate.

The historical momentum and its specificity from Aeneas to Romulus' race (*gente*, another lexical allusion to the notion of begetting) lead immediately to Rome's latest "rebirth" and to Augustus, and it is a suitable moment for the emperor himself to enter the poem (49–52):

> Quaeque vos bobus veneratur albis
> clarus Anchisae Venerisque sanguis,
> impetret, bellante prior, iacentem
> > lenis in hostem.

> And what the glorious scion of Anchises and Venus asks of you, with [the sacrifice of] white steers, may he obtain, superior to his warring [foe], gentle to the fallen enemy.

We are suddenly back to Troy again, through the mating of Anchises and Venus, but we are also equally placed in the Rome of
17 B.C.E. where we find the new Aeneas, the descendant of god
and mortal, reiterating the same role as his semi-divine ancestor,
as he presides over the moment of renewal.

First a word on location. If we combine information from
both the Sibylline oracle and the *Acta* inscription, we learn that
white cattle were sacrificed on the Capitoline by Augustus and
Agrippa, bulls to Jupiter on June 1, cows to Juno on the second.
Although the oracle speaks of Apollo as due to receive the same
sacrifice as Jupiter and Juno,[55] there is no mention in the *Acta* of
animal offerings to Apollo and Diana on June 3, only of cakes,
nine each of three varieties presented to both divinities. This has
led critics, with reason, to interpret the repeated *di* of lines 45–
46 as including Jupiter and Juno, which in turn would co-opt
the Olympic pantheon into the poet's apostrophe. The result,
which also has been duly noted, suggests that Horace's poem,
in its role as climax of the triduum of festivities, would have us
survey the events as a whole and incorporate at the least the king
and queen of heaven, who had been the special foci of the rites
on the two preceding days, into his concluding celebratory song.
Nevertheless by leaving his *di* here anonymous, he not only absorbs all divine power into his prayer, he also gives particular
force to Apollo and Diana who are the recipients of the poem
and whose naming, at beginning, center, and finale, gives it its
principal structure.[56]

Again etymological wordplay lends a special dynamism to the
poet's language. From Plautus on Latin authors have made use
of the connection between *Venus* and *veneror*,[57] and Horace himself links the final poems of his fourth book of odes by having
venerantur and *Veneris* in their respective concluding lines.[58] The
figuration has special point here because it unites Augustus'
prayer, and implicitly himself, with his divine ancestress. His

prayer and its proclamation contain, as it were, the force of his inherited, and innate, divinity. Nor is Anchises absent from the poet's verbal play. If Venus dominates the stanza's relative clause, Anchises is present in the main verb, *impetret*, whose etymology, based on the word *pater*, indicates the completion of a request such as a *pater familias* might have posed. Aeneas/Augustus' "father" is thus also part of the total prayer, now not in the asking but in the gaining. Just as, in terms of human genealogy, Venus and Anchises were the parents of Aeneas and therefore dynamic ancestors of his modern reincarnation, so they share in the lexical heritage, and therefore in the forcefulness, of the prayer that Augustus is offering. Birth is again much on Horace's mind, whether it be the origin of Aeneas and Augustus, the source of the language with which Horace enfolds them, or the potential of the combination to help realize the hymn's entreaty.

The invocation tendered by the emperor, of which we learn only vicariously, joins the poem's other "languages," of the Sibyl and of the Parcae, to form a major subsidiary of Horace's utterance. His prayer is complemented by, just as it incorporates, theirs as further agents of the *Carmen*'s comprehensive strength. The poet, through the word *lenis*, also grants Augustus the incipient apotheosis that he has bestowed on Aeneas by means of the implications of *daturus*. *Lenis* returns us to line 14 and to the "gentleness" of Diana/Ilithyia to those in childbirth. Augustus verbally gains a parallel to the recipient of the hymn, but his *lenitas* looks not to human engendering but to the political and military preservation of Rome and its citizens. If Diana's mildness is toward the immediate, literal births that will guarantee Rome's future, Augustus' *lenitas* finds its implementation in the clemency that is a signpost of his country's ethical renewal. The emperor is as gentle to his humbled enemies as the goddess is to Roman mothers in travail. And if gentleness links Augustus with Diana, the mere fact of being temperate toward one's foes connects Augustus with his patron god Apollo, "with his arrow replaced in his quiver" (*condito telo,* 33), that is, with war or at least civil conflict a thing of the past. He is the mortal equivalent of his immortal overseer, but the parallelism suggests that Augustus, as the terrestrial embodiment of Apollo, shares in his divinity as well.

The language in which this *lenitas* is couched has a further, special referentiality in this context. Commentators in glossing the larger phrase *bellante prior, iacentem / lenis in hostem* point rightly to the *Aeneid* and to the concluding words of Anchises' splendid disquisition to Aeneas on the future of Rome. At this moment of climax Virgil has father extend to son the poem's most famous ethical dictum. Addressing him as *Romane,* that is, as prototype, or even representative, of his race to come, Anchises asks him "to spare those made subject and subdue the proud through war."[59] But it is well to consider here, in the intellectual context we have been tracing, Horace's careful allusion to the epic masterpiece of his contemporary and friend.

Mention of Aeneas as *superstes patriae* could be taken as Horace's initial bow to father as well as fatherland, but it is the direct naming of Anchises, supplemented by the *figura etymologica* in *impetret,* that further confirms the allusion to the *Aeneid.* Anchises receives the epithet *pater* eighteen times in the epic. It is as father that we see him in, and remember him from, the poem. And it is in this same role that his words ring out again through Horace's remembrance. The fatherhood of Anchises strengthens the equation of Augustus with Aeneas, himself styled *pater* with equal regularity throughout his epic. The new Aeneas, as Horace would have us imagine the emperor, both absorbs and puts into practice the ethical inheritance of Anchises in a way that Virgil does not allow his hero fully to implement in the course of his epic.[60]

The implications of Anchises' words spill over into the next stanza as Horace, in two quatrains, turns to examining the "now" of postwar Rome (53–60):

iam mari terraque manus potentis
Medus Albanasque timet securis,
iam Scythae responsa petunt, superbi
       nuper et Indi.

iam Fides et Pax et Honos Pudorque
priscus et neglecta redire Virtus
audet adparetque beata pleno
       Copia cornu.

Now the Parthian fears our troops, lords of sea and land, and the axes of Alba, now the Scythians and the Indi, haughty until recently, seek answers [from us]. Now Fidelity and Peace and Honor and ancient Modesty and neglected Courage dare to return, and blessed Plenty, with full horn, makes her appearance.

Horace carefully finesses the universality of Anchises' apothegm, applicable to civic violence at home as well as to warring abroad, by attaching the epithet *superbus* now strictly to Rome's foreign enemies who under Augustus sue for her understanding. The lyric poet leaves behind the problematics of civil strife that Virgil demands we face when pondering Aeneas' arrival in Italy to establish power over the Latins and their chief defender Turnus. The epic poet was too close to the final siege of domestic war, leading up to Actium, and to the ambiguities of Octavian's conflict with Antony and Cleopatra not to have it suffuse his text. In the contemporary literature, the Egyptian queen was often portrayed as a foreign courtesan bent on becoming ruler of Rome with the aid of her barbaric minions. Antony, Roman nobleman once married to the future emperor's sister, was not so easily characterized as alien.

At one extraordinary moment in his epic dealing with the tradition of opening and closing of the *Belli portae*, Virgil distinguishes clearly the two types of warfare with which Rome has been deeply embroiled for more than a century. In the "now" (*nunc*) of future Augustan glory, as Virgil sees it, Rome's citizens make war only against foreign enemies:[61]

> sive Getis inferre manu lacrimabile bellum
> Hyrcanisve Arabisve parant, seu tendere ad Indos
> Auroramque sequi Parthosque reposcere signa . . .

> whether their hands are preparing to bring tearful war to the Getae, or to the Hyrcani or Arabes, or to march against the Indi and follow the dawn and demand back their standards from the Parthi.

In the poem's present, when king Latinus refuses to declare war against Aeneas and the gates are finally bashed in by furious Juno, we find ourselves immersed in a civil conflict that ends as the poem concludes with a far from gentle Aeneas ferociously plunging his sword into the chest of his suppliant foe. Horace's *Carmen* would construct a Rome different from Virgil's imagining of the future. Not only is Rome's omnipotent ruler gentle under all circumstances, he also does not need to declare foreign wars since Rome's enemies sue for peace.

The presence of the *Aeneid* may also be felt in the phrase *Albanas securis*. This is the only occasion in Horace's poetry where the adjective *Albanus* refers not to the Alban hills per se but by metonymy both to an essential historical development in the accretion of power to the Romans and as a stand-in for contemporary Roman might. The *Albani patres* of the opening of the *Aeneid*[62] have yielded to Horace's *Albanas securis* so that Alba Longa has become not just a way station in the evolution of Rome, a moment of importance, in Virgil's depiction, between *genus Latinum* and *altae moenia Romae,* but also a crucial component of Roman jurisdictional authority as she extends her dominion over those hitherto resistant to her sway.

In sum, fourteen years after Augustus confirmed his authority with the decisive victory at Actium and two after Virgil's death and the presumed publication of the *Aeneid,* Horace can look at Roman might, and at the emperor who stands as its primary incorporation, with less ambiguous eyes than his late colleague or, better, can imagine *inclementia* and the negative aspects of pride away from Rome. *Superbia* now brings its taint only to Rome's unconquered enemies. The phrase *responsa petunt* turns Rome not just into the source of presumed gratification to her petitioners but also into a quasi-oracular divinity, capable, Sibyl-like, of announcing their *fata* to those who have come under her sway.[63] Horace allows Rome, now implicitly divine like its leader, no room or need for vengeance.

The anaphora of *iam* links lines 57–60 with the preceding stanza, but when Horace turns from the foreign to the domestic situation of present Rome, he carefully places us in a world of abstractions. In dealing with Rome's aspirations to dominate its antagonists abroad it is proper to name names, to pit Alban axes against haughty Scythians. In moving to the city's spiritual world he need invoke no specifics, not even the pattern-setting *castitas* of Aeneas or Augustus' *lenitas.* Cases of individual ethical heroism, however paradigmatic, that Roman history has produced in its course give place fully to the personified virtues that now rule society. Nor need Horace allude to past moral problems here any more than to civil war in the preceding stanza. It is enough for him to mention the return of Pax for his audience to realize that they happily now find themselves in a postwar period with civil strife a matter of the past. The other abstractions bear the same pointed weight. Fides — trust and good faith — is allied with Honor in that both are concerned with the solemnity of agreements, here of a people and of its individual citizens among themselves. Honor also looks to esteem due military heroism and thus is closely allied with Virtus (they shared a temple at the Porta Capena). But the renewed worship of Virtus after a period of disregard does not mean the absence of courage in recent Roman history, only its misuse by those appropriating innate Roman martial vigor for the purposes of fratricide.

Hence Horace's particular stress on the enjambed *Pudor priscus*. In *Aeneid* 6 Anchises singles out the *prisca Fides* of young Marcellus for special praise.[64] The implications here are clear enough. The restoration of ancient Pudor, of Shame before one's fellow citizens and of the decency in moral behavior that this suggests, presumes its absence in the recent Roman past. But with the advent of the *Pax Augusta,* mutual Trust can be restored, Courage and its concomitant Honor can be reinstated as ethical values (but with their martial potential available only against foreign foes), and Shame, awareness of how one's actions are judged by others and of the need for their moral approbation, revived after a period of moral decline when the body politic was at odds with itself. In this poem of renewals and restorations Horace once again sends us back to Roman spiritual beginnings.

With the advent of Copia with her full horn we are also in a period of reinvigorated earthly bounty. Cornucopia is a standard symbol of the Golden Age and therefore appropriate to join with Tellus and Ceres as harbingers of nature's return to a time of generosity. In this context the word *adparet* has special significance. It has the effect of personifying Copia and her abundance. It also imparts something not only of the brilliance of the Augustan moment but yet again of the power of the poet's song to conjure its particularities into being. The epiphany of Copia may be a fitting complement to the emperor's revitalization of Rome's spiritual life and betoken a return to its sturdy origins, but it also is a manifestation of the poet's magical power as executed in the chanting of his singers.

These lines, like lines 17–20 on the decrees of the fathers, have been found wanting, one critic calling them "frigid," with generalities that appear "artificial."[65] In terms of the poem's intricate balances, however, the abstractions are best seen as correspondents to the list formed by Tellus, Ceres, and Jupiter at 29–32. Certainly Copia, with her horn of plenty, has close associations in Augustan iconography especially with the figure of Earth.[66] Just as the initial list of divinities blessing Rome's fertility immediately precedes the apostrophes that round off the poem's first half, so the second comes just before the final references to Apollo and Diana.

But the differences between the two rosters help illustrate something of Horace's purposes as the poem runs its course. Lines 29–32, as we have seen, present concrete gods, female and male, associated with earth, air, and water who assure the city's agricultural prosperity and therefore confirm the tangible setting for her renewal. Lines 57–60, by contrast, form part of the climax that began with the entrance of history into the poem, leading from the birth of Rome under Aeneas to its refoundation under Aeneas' descendant, Augustus. But these figures, however consequential as specific leaders in Rome's advance to greatness, also embody the moral abstractions that guarantee her ethical as well as physical reinvigoration. Their attendance is the crowning accolade to the continuity of model exemplars that the history of Rome has occasioned. It is both a credit to Rome, and a bow to the magical capabilities of the *Carmen*, that these abstractions now make their appearance as palpably present to the worshippers. They are as vital to her spiritual future as Tellus is to her external well-being.[67]

As the poem draws to conclusion we turn back to its honorands, here, to round matters off, allotted the same nomenclature they received at the poem's start (61–72):

> Augur et fulgente decorus arcu
> Phoebus acceptusque novem Camenis
> qui salutari levat arte fessos
>   corporis artus,
>
> si Palatinas videt aequos aras,
> remque Romanam Latiumque felix
> alterum in lustrum meliusque semper
>   prorogat aevum,
>
> quaeque Aventinum tenet Algidumque,
> quindecim Diana preces virorum
> curat et votis puerorum amicas
>   adplicat auris.

> Phoebus, prophet both graced with his gleaming bow and dear to the nine Muses, who with his saving art relieves the body's tired limbs, if he views with favor the altars on the Palatine, always prolongs Roman strength and the prosperity of Latium for a further cycle and to a better age, and Diana, who holds Aventine and Algidus, gives heed to the prayers of the Fifteen and lends friendly ears to the appeals of the youth.[68]

In the initial stanzas of the poem, Apollo as Sol was allotted the third quatrain while the subsequent two were devoted to Diana/Ilithyia. (The first stanza and the ninth, as we have seen, were assigned to both divinities and framed the ode's initial half.) Here at the conclusion the balance is redressed, with Apollo serving as focus for two stanzas and Diana for one.[69]

Apollo is visualized in terms of four of his major roles, as god of prophecy, hunting and war, music and poetry, and disease and health. All attributes look back into the poem. His *salutari . . . arte* reminds us of Jupiter's *aquae salubres* (31) and of the value of good health to a nation's well-being. The gleaming bow with which the god is adorned recalls not only his initial appearance as part of *lucidum caeli decus* (2) but also the *telum* (30) that in the new dispensation will remain in its quiver. The god's armory, in other words, is still worthy of contemplation as a reminder of his physical prowess, but it now serves more as a sign of grace than of energy released. His status as a god of prophecy is fitting for a poem that anticipates his share in prolonging this glorious moment and for a poet gifted with the capacity to anticipate it. Finally there is the god's position as musagète.[70] Again its appositeness to Horace's present inspiration to produce charming song needs no underlining. The extent of Apollo's dynamism is suitably brought before us toward the end of a masterful effort of the poetic imagination. It functions as confirmatory preparation for the poet's subsequent direct statement of what the god (and his mouthpiece) now actually accomplish.

Each detail in the god's litany would have also resonated, in a practical fashion, with its contemporary audience. The epithet *augur*, which Horace had already applied to the god at *c.* 1. 2. 32, connects Apollo as god of prophecy and prophets with the new Rome from whom once unconquered territories now "seek responses" (*responsa petunt,* 55). More specifically, Apollo as Augur would be connected with the shrine of Roma Quadrata, located *ante templum Apollonis* and therefore neighboring the temple complex on the Palatine where this segment of the *Ludi* was being carried out.[71] Finally, Suetonius in his life of Augustus explicitly associates the name given the emperor in 27 with *augurium,* quoting Ennius as his authority for the etymologizing:[72]

> ... Augusto augurio postquam incluta condita
>> [Roma est.

after glorious Rome had been founded by august augury.

The epithet Augur, therefore, connects Apollo not only with his Palatine temple and the place for receiving auguries associated with it but also, first, with Romulus, establisher of Rome itself and likewise dweller on the Palatine, near the emperor's own residence, who took the famous augury at the initiation of her history, and second, most prominently with Rome's august reestablisher who took Apollo as his patron god.[73]

Next we visualize Apollo as "graced with his gleaming bow" (*fulgente decorus arcu*), a reminder of the complex, symbolic power of his bow but also of his and his sister's appearance in the poem as "brilliant grace of heaven" (*lucidum caeli decus*). Reference to the god's physical beauty as well as to his bow again helps us position ourselves before the Palatine temple, which had two statues of Apollo associated with it. The first was in the courtyard, the second, as noted before, was placed within the temple. If we may trust the evidence of Propertius, in both Apollo is depicted as *citharoedus:* that is, as god of song.[74]

The connection with music continues into the next characterization of Apollo, namely, that he is "dear to the nine Muses" (*acceptus . . . novem Camenis*). By using Camenae here instead of Musae, Horace links Apollo not only with specifically Roman patronesses of song and singer but with the word *carmen* itself, with the great ode to which poet and audience are bearing witness and with poetic creativity in general. This in turn serves to recall Apollo's intimacy with the Greek and Latin libraries conjoined to his shrine. Already in the first book of epistles, published three years before the *Ludi* took place, Horace can refer to "whichever writings Palatine Apollo has received" (*scripta Palatinus quaecumque recepit Apollo*), using the adjective *Palatinus* for the only other occasion in his poetry outside the *Carmen*.[75] Horace twice elsewhere connects Apollo and his temple with the libraries and with poetry-making. The first allusion is directed to Augustus, asking him to attend to readers and reading "if you wish to fill with books that gift worthy of Apollo."[76] The second, addressed most likely to the same (Julius) Florus who is the recipient of *epistle* 1. 3, speaks of the shrine "now open to Roman bards."[77]

The final characteristic in this summation of Apolline power is the god's association with the healing arts. Although Apollo Medicus has no specific connection with his complex on the Palatine, he is the dedicatee of the temple *in Circo* restored by Gaius Sosius in 32 and adjacent to the theater named for Marcellus, who died in 23, where Greek stage plays were performed during the *Ludi*.[78] The temple plays a significant role in our understanding of Augustan iconography. As for Sosius, although he fought on Antony's side at the battle of Actium, he was pardoned by Augustus and served as one of the *Quindecimviri* in charge of performing the *Ludi* whose prayers figure in the *Carmen*'s penultimate stanza.[79]

The final quatrain devoted to Apollo and the opening of the final verses devoted to Diana expand our mental vision both topographically and temporally. Our eyes, along with Apollo's, are for one last time centered on the Palatine and on the altars in front of the temple. But, while we recall the *res Romana* (47) for which the chorus has previously prayed as part of its petitions on behalf of the *gens Romula*, our sight travels, first to Diana's Aventine and then to the remaining five hills, emblems of the city as a whole. Our line of vision extends further to *Latium felix* and to its Mount Algidus, equally sacred to Diana. Such a spatial broadening, if we join it to what the poem has previously displayed, allows us to follow the enlargement of *res Romana* itself from small beginnings on the banks of the Tiber to the lands of the Scythae and Indi, now craving peace.

Topographical expansion is complemented by extension of time from present into the distant future. Horace has touched on many aspects of temporality in the *Carmen*. He has placed us in the eternal time of the gods and their celestial equivalents, sun and moon. We have watched the individual human time of adolescent choristers and of the continuum of birth, youth, marriage, and old age that is their particular lot. There is the specific moment of the festival celebration, with its days and nights. This culminates in the here and now of June 3, 17 B.C.E., but the chronology reminds us that what we are witnessing is the descendant of similar festivities whose repetition harks back well into the Roman past. Likewise we take careful cognizance of a different stretch of Roman historical time, which takes us from Troy to Rome or, put in terms of personages, from Aeneas, son of Venus and Anchises, to Romulus and finally to Augustus. Time passes and brings mutation of events and of the people who distinguish them. But there is recurrence, too, not only of the *Ludi* but of the begetters and saviors of Rome who founded her and bring her renewal.

Augustus, like Aeneas, has been through his time of trial and, so we would presume, is prepared like his prototype to serve as a model of *castitas* for Rome's docile youth. Historical temporality thus merges with what we might call Sibylline time, the cyclic chronology oriented toward the *saeculum*, an ongoing, positive progression that is yet concerned with returns and reinvigorations.[80] Rome's narrative, in Apollo's hands, will continue on for another *lustrum*, for five further years and another moment of purgation. But Rome will also prosper into a still vaguer, more extensive *aevum*, a better, more enduring age to come. Finally, with the word *semper*, Rome is foreseen as participating in the atemporal eternity of the immortals. Apollo asks this of Rome and we have known of it from the start of the poem (*semper*, 3).

The final detailed look at Diana extends our vision first across the valley of the Circus Maximus to the Aventine and thence to the range of mountains east of the city. But it also leaves us with the specifics of prayer. If *semper* in the preceding stanza brings our thoughts back to the poem's opening lines, mention of the *Quindecimviri sacris faciundis*, who were in charge of consulting and implementing the cryptic sayings of the Sibyl, turns our attention once more to the *Sibyllini versus* of line 5 and to the actuality of the festival for which they called. It is a curious matter of fact, promoting the inclusivity of the occasion, that the virgin goddess lends her ears specifically to men, to the solemn priests managing the proceedings and to the youths in the chorus, singing their prayers.[81]

Universality is likewise a critical element as we turn to the poem's conclusion and back to the chorus itself (73–76):

> Haec Iovem sentire deosque cunctos
> spem bonam certamque domum reporto,
> doctus et Phoebi chorus et Dianae
>   dicere laudes.

> That Jupiter and all the gods pay heed to these [words] I bear home good and assured hope, I the chorus taught to tell the praises of Phoebus and of Diana.

All the gods are made to share in realizing the chorus' prayers, but Apollo and Diana appropriately receive the last word, sealing the poem and completing its own special cycle by leading us back to the double apostrophe of line 1 just as the concluding phrase *dicere laudes* revives the last line of the opening address (*dicere carmen*, 8). Song and the praises it contains have coalesced into a unity through the poet's words.[82]

There is, however, one subtle but interesting alteration from the beginning in the conclusion. The "we" of the singers in their initial prayer (*precamur*, 3), though through its resonance with *preces* it is a prominent element in the poem's satisfying circularity, becomes at the end the "I" of a chorus bringing home the goodwill of the gods. The discrete elements of the many individuals who make up the group meld into one all-subsuming "I" as the group stands for the totality of Rome before the gods. But, even while advancing this singularity through the moving phrase *domum reporto*, the poet has his chorus also prepare to splinter again into the unique identities of its constituent members. After their collective moment in the limelight they are about to become again individuated parts of fifty-four Roman households, bringing with them the blessings that have accrued from their roles as liaisons between men and gods.

In this context, especially at the poem's end, the word *doctus* takes on particular significance because it brings in Horace himself, the teacher who trains the chorus to be his spokesman. But can the Horatian lyric "I," which readers of the poet's work last heard in the magnificent vaunt of *exegi monumentum aere perennius*, be considered totally absorbed in the public, universal utterance of the *Carmen?* How differentiated is the "I" of the chorus *(reporto)* from the "I" we are used to from the regular speaker of Horatian lyric? The *doctus chorus* stands in part for the *docilis iuventa* (45), the youth of Rome, who will learn renewed morality just as the chorus learns the words that will help bring it about. But the chorus, as students honoring their teacher, also presumably gives voice to the thoughts of the "I" behind its words. Apollo and Diana may inspire, and Augustus commission, but the poem's creator is Horace. Rome is the gods' *opus*, but the poem, and therefore the Rome recreated in and by the poem, is the *monumentum* of the poet monumentalizing Rome.[83]

Horace's subliminal self-presentation comes more to the surface if we look at other aspects of the narrative technique in the final stanzas. Two characteristics of the concluding mentions of Apollo and Diana in lines 61–72 are unexpected. The first is the complete absence of apostrophe. The chorus turns to the two gods at their last appearance in the ode not with the *tu*-form of hymnic address, with vocatives that might form the capstone of its imprecation or with a synopsis of attributes.[84] In the place of a final direct address expected in a hymn's summation we have only the innuendo of third person narrative. Concomitant with this change of salutation is the yielding of the subjunctives and imperatives associated with prayer to indicatives, and of future orientation to present. The present indicatives—*prorogat, curat* and *adplicat*—no longer project requests or commands that batten on hope but describe events in the process of occurring. Divine supplication and exhortation yield to declarative statements as the gods appear, in the poet's rhetoric, to be carrying out the goals for whose implementation the chorus had earlier appealed. The source of power is not now the chorus but the magic song that it has been taught to chant. The author of the *Carmen*, through his verbal sorcery, has brought the previous prayers to fruition.

In fact, the present indicatives, and the replacement of prayer by assertion of faits accomplis, begin immediately after Augustus enters the poem and the chorus asks that the gods grant whatever the new Aeneas entreats of them. Suddenly the Parthian now fears the strength of Rome and Plenty renews her epiphany. It is as if Augustus' special requests of the gods had forthwith been answered and their efficacy proven by the prosperity of Rome both at home and abroad. But the emperor's prayers in fact form only one particular part of the *energeia* of the poem. Augustus is a crucial figure in realizing the productive plan of the gods for Rome, but it is the poet who recreates Augustus and his orisons and who announces their accomplishment, all through the seduction of poetry. It is Horace who sees for us with immediacy and clarity the realization that the imagination's rituals create and who displays them before us. Finally, it is he who fulfills not only the prayers of Augustus but the verses of the Sibyl and the chantings of the Fates, incorporating them into his still grander imaginative gesture. Once more Rome and Augustus are his dependents, brought into being and secure in the god's blessing through the poet's magic.

The authority to which Horace thus lays claim is enormous. To represent through a poet's verses the condition of Rome in 17 B.C.E., be it visualized through the details of a particular ceremony occurring on June 3 on the Palatine hill or through any of several more expansive glimpses of her situation, is to enact and affirm it. Such a proclamation of mastery, where words manufacture deeds and tangible is pronounced and enforced through intangible, gains crucial justification from the very self-presentation of the poet's deed. He not only devises a poem meant initially for immediate public appreciation, he also in person directs its performance. He thus could be said to create Rome for his contemporaries as well as for us, who stand for any later ratifiers of her quality.

For all these reasons it is important to remember that the singing of the *Carmen Saeculare* came as the crowning point of the three days of ritual that were the religious core of the *Ludi*. Although not explicitly part of the sacrificial rites themselves, the Song not only was their crucial appendage but gave assurance of their value, not least as manifested through the change we traced in its course from supplicatory hymn to odic pronouncement of matters achieved. Performance of the *Ludi Saeculares* signalized the end of one *saeculum* and celebrated the beginning of another. The triduum of ceremonies formed the grand finale of the solemn exercises that Horace's poem in turn climactically ratified. The end of the religious part of the *Ludi* and its concluding song are contemporaneous, but it is the poet's special power that assures the coming-true of prayers to fulfill the purposes of the *Ludi* themselves. One of these prayers, unspoken by Horace but doubtless on the minds of the emperor as of all his subjects, was that the new *saeculum* of one hundred and ten years be different from the last and that especially the physical and moral destructiveness of civil war be a thing of the past.

I would like now to test the originality of the *Carmen* as hymn, first by looking at the challenges Horace had set for himself by comparison to his earlier lyric prayers, then by examining the effect of the *Carmen* on his later odes, an effect the poet himself makes central to the understanding of *c.* 4. 6.

4

Horatian Hymn and the
Carmen Saeculare

Let us turn now to Horace's poetic output before and after the *Carmen Saeculare*. In this chapter I will first survey the hymns or hymnlike odes in the first three books, in particular *c.* 1. 21, and then examine Horace's reaction to the presentation of the *Carmen*, especially as documented in the extraordinary sixth ode of the fourth book.

A comparison of the *Carmen Saeculare* with the dozen or so complete, partial, or parodic hymns in the initial collection of odes confirms the several special qualities of the *Carmen*, not least the uniqueness of its final sextet of quatrains. In none of Horace's other hymns do present tenses, without apostrophe or adherence to second person address, occur as evidence that the ode's prayers are in fact in the process of being fulfilled. As I have noted, the chorus as narrator concludes its work by stating what the gods now are doing. There is no need, after the double salutation to *di* at 45–46, thirty lines before the poem's conclusion, of any further invocation through direct speech, whether through use of the *tu-* formula or of the vocative.

As a focus for analogy between the earlier lyrics and the *Carmen* we might look again at *c.* 1. 21, Horace's only other ode both linking Apollo and Diana together and, as is also the case with the *Carmen*, involving a double chorus of girls and boys. In the earlier ode, the first group is to sing of the virgin goddess who delights in nature and, in particular, in the mountains of Latium (Algidus, as in the *Carmen*), Arcadia, and Lycia. The second is to praise Tempe, Delos, and the god of the quiver and the lyre. It is he alone who claims the final stanza with its announcement that Apollo will shunt off war, hunger, and disease from Rome and its Caesar and onto foreign enemies east and north.

One of the salient differences between the two poems that might help us point up Horace's specific purposes in the *Carmen,* is that Apollo is given prominence over his sister in the earlier poem whereas in the *Carmen* both are treated with virtually equal emphasis. The earlier ode is in fact not a hymn at all but the directions for a hymn's performance with the narrator as teacher and chorus leader in the rhetorical foreground of the poem. Commands (*dicite, dicite, tollite*) are directed not immediately at the gods through the act of prayer but on the incipient performers of the hymn as they are trained for their task. The boys, naturally enough, are to concentrate on Apollo, the girls on Diana.

We are given no clue of any such division in the *Carmen.* The difficulty of the task before those who would divide stanzas between boys and girls according to what is considered suitable subject matter or would apportion the stanzas antiphonally between the sexes or would even envision some stanzas sung in unison, some not, is compounded by the fact that the number of quatrains is odd, not even (19).[1] Horace, as we have seen, grants "we" to the chorus at the poem's beginning, "I" at the end, but never "we boys" or "we girls." A sense of universality remains, missing in *c.* 1. 21 with its manifest pedagogy.

By comparison with *c* 1. 21, the *Carmen* dispenses with obliqueness. The singers, unmediated by a teacher who pronounces on content and presentation, address the gods directly from the start of the poem, and their entreaty is fulfilled in the present. Apollo is now prolonging the amelioration of Rome, Diana is in the very act of caring for her suppliants. It is as if Horace, in accepting Augustus' commission and in displaying in public his sympathy for the emperor and his Rome, eliminated any indirection in narrative technique as a way of signaling this unfettered approval. Nothing stands between his chorus and their gods or between himself and Augustus' aims for the physical and moral betterment of Rome.

Finally there is the question of subject matter. Let me quote again the earlier ode's last stanza in full:

> hic bellum lacrimosum, hic miseram famem
>   pestemque a populo et principe Caesare in
>   Persas atque Britannos
>   vestra motus aget prece.

> Moved by your prayer, he [Apollo] will drive tearful war, will drive sad hunger and disease from the people and Caesar their prince onto the Persians and the Britons.

The magic of Horace's singers and their song here is more than apotropaic. To ask the god to ward off war, famine, and pestilence from Rome is to imply their active, vitiating presences as well as the possibility of averting their menace. Both content and tone of the *Carmen* are different. Although there is allusion to war, it is treated as a thing of the past, and Horace's stress on fertility and productivity precludes any mention of their opposites. The *Carmen Saeculare* is not a prayer to turn aside evil or mitigate the gods' displeasure. It is a hymn to confirm by incantation the glory of the Roman status quo.

Horace was justly proud of his accomplishment in writing and, as it were, producing the *Carmen*. This sense of achievement surfaces on several occasions in his poetry written after 17. We feel it vicariously in the joyous boastfulness that pervades *c. 4. 3.*[2] Horace is now ranked by the offspring of princely Rome "among the lovable choruses of bards" (*inter amabilis vatum . . .*

choros, 14–15) and pointed out by the finger of those passing by as the "player of the Roman lyre" (*Romanae fidicen lyrae*, 23). His role as seer-bard-poetic wizard for Rome is now assured as is his particular repute as Rome's supreme lyricist.

But Horace's most immediate, detailed mention of the *Carmen* in his last lyric collection takes place in its sixth ode.[3] This powerful, deeply moving poem draws toward its conclusion by a direct address to the choristers themselves of the *Carmen*, asking them to watch his beat as they duly sing the praises of Apollo and Diana. He ends by quoting the words of one of the female singers, imagined now on the point of marriage (41–44):

> nupta iam dices "ego dis amicum,
> saeculo festas referente luces,
> reddidi carmen docilis modorum
>   vatis Horati."

> Now when a bride you will proclaim: "As the age was restoring days of celebration, I myself rendered a song friendly to the gods, I, instructed in the modes of the bard, Horace."

Not only is a member of the chorus particularized, appropriately for the tone of the *Carmen* at the time of her wedding, now the poet can also directly name himself in a way the self-effacement demanded by the public ceremony could not allow, as bard and chorus master is absorbed into the chorus that itself stands as synecdoche for the Roman populace. It is the individual genius, Quintus Horatius Flaccus, who can some four years later exult in the patent efficacy of his song.

Yet he, too, has a patron, the god Apollo. In the *Carmen* he had shared honors with his twin, Diana. Here, though the goddess is twice mentioned in connection with the chorus and its task, it is the god of the bow and the lyre who remains the poem's primary addressee and focal figure. It is he who is teacher of the poet, the defender of the specialness of his muse (the Latin *Camena*, 27), the bestower of inspiration (*spiritum*, 29), the art of song (*artem carminis*, 29–30), and reputation (*nomen*, 30). The lyre's god (*fidicen*, 25, the word Horace had used of himself in *c.* 4. 3) is the fitting teacher-benefactor (*doctor*, 25) of Rome's lyre player who in turn makes his own pupil *docilis* (43), a clear reminder of *docili iuventae* (*C. S.* 45) and *doctus chorus* (*C. S.* 75). But the god has a past as well as a creative present, and the poem's first five stanzas dwell on a particular aspect of that past, which helps distinguish both this earlier Apollo from the god of the *Carmen* and *c.* 4. 6 from the great song of whose performance it tells.

Although *C.* 4. 6 is shorter than the *Carmen*, it is in one respect structured along similar lines: its central stanza also takes us on the journey west from Troy by mention of "the affairs of Aeneas" (*rebus Aeneae*, 23) and the walls (*muros*, 24) of Rome that will arise as its result. The entrance of history through Rome's founding father and its fortifications is pivotal to each poem. But the mention of *muros* as the heritage of Aeneas strikes a note that jars with the tone of the *Carmen*, which sees Rome only in terms of its hills (*colles*) in general, and the Palatine, site of Apollo's temple with its altars, and Diana's Aventine in particular. Rome's bellicosity is suppressed in favor of sacrality and of a special ceremony that ensures the city's rejuvenation and spiritual health.

The initial five stanzas of *c.* 4. 6 offer a still more startling discrepancy from the first half of the *Carmen*. Horace begins his later ode with a detailed presentation of Apollo as god of vengeance, first against Niobe (the subject displayed on one of his temple's doors) and Tityos, but primarily against Achilles whose malevolent heroism, which even extended to viciousness toward captives and pregnant women, is no match for the god's prowess.

Horace gives us a different Apollo from the one who is a primary subject of the *Carmen*, presiding over Rome's rebirth as leader of the Muses more than as master of the bow. But not only is the militarism of Apollo downplayed in the *Carmen*, there is no mention of his propensity for reprisal (or, for that matter, of Augustus' fixation with revenge), though Horace has ample opportunity to claim it for our attention.

There are specific and general reasons for Horace in the *Carmen* to avoid both noting this aspect of Apollo and, in particular, calling attention to Achilles. But the elaborate reference to both topics, which is to say the reintroduction into literature of vengeful Apollo as well as renewed emphasis on bloodthirsty Achilles, in *c.* 4. 6, a poem so closely concerned with the creation and production of the *Carmen*, asks us to ponder the reasons for their absence in the public ode. The general cause takes us back again into the intellectual history we will shortly trace from the sixty-fourth poem of Catullus and Virgil's fourth *eclogue* to the *Carmen*. In the first poem Achillean savagery is a mark of the transition between an age when gods were imminent in the affairs of mortals and a time of human decadence when our immorality precluded the presence of divinity. Achilles also makes a brief appearance in *eclogue* 4 where his conduct offers evidence for a period of war, which mankind must experience again, as the poem's remarkable child develops into manhood but before the new age's happy apogee.

Achilles, in the poetic background of the *Carmen*, thus stands for war's violence to which Augustus' golden present need not have recourse now that civil battling is over and that Rome's antagonists abroad have experienced her strength. For this alone Achilles could not appear in the *Carmen*. But there is a still more specific reason. Achilles was the supreme hero of the Greeks in their fighting against the Trojans, and when Aeneas and his countrymen are translated into Augustus and Rome, the Greeks and their leader, from one point of view,[4] become not some foreign foe but Rome's own internal adversaries during a time of fraternal strife, adversaries whose latest leader, from an Augustan perspective, would be Antony. But fratricidal warfare can find no place in a *Carmen* that celebrates Rome's rebirth in a time of opulence. And here Apollo reenters the picture.

The change from Apollo as retributive divinity to inspirer of the *Carmen* is the ideological nub of *c.* 4. 6. By restoring vindictive Apollo and murderous Achilles to our attention in the later ode, which remains in essence a "history" of the *Carmen*'s genesis and reception, Horace is in fact laying bare the processes of their purgation from the Song itself. These alterations are important for Horace as he puts the creation of the *Carmen* into the more expansive portrayal of the period of transition from Actium to the *Ludi Saeculares*. Apollo, in Virgil's vision, presides over Actium[5] and, for all Augustus' ameliorating efforts to diminish the civil aspects of the conflict with Antony, it was as a god of revenge that the emperor chose to depict him on the doors of his monumental Palatine temple. In describing allegorically the circumstances of Actium in *c.* 4. 6, Horace takes due note of Apollo-Augustus both as vindicator of past wrongs and in particular as killer of his archenemy Achilles, who incorporates, as Horace would see it, the worst aspects of martial violence.

However patent Horace may be in *c.* 4. 6 as he places the inspiration for the *Carmen* in its historical and intellectual setting, in the *Carmen* itself the bellicose aura of Apollo and Augustus must be minimized and relegated to the past. Likewise Achilles, multivalent symbol of Greece fighting Troy, of opposition to Augustus (and perhaps even of the latter's tendencies toward vengeance), and of war's barbarism in general, must now be suppressed entirely. The particular poetic tradition dealing with Achilles, therefore, that takes him from Catullus 64 and thence to Virgil's fourth *eclogue* and *Aeneid* assumes two forms in Horace's post-*Aeneid* reinventions. In *c.* 4. 6 Horace's "I" becomes the final protagonist of the poem, transposing Apollo from his role of *vindex* to that of *doctor,* teacher and protector of the inspired *vatis* who can begin by detailing the brutality of Achilles against the unborn and end with a young wife vaunting her part in singing the *Carmen.* Achilles is a crucial ingredient in this progress, to be named by a poet and disposed of by a warrior god who is also a prompter of bards. In the *Carmen,* however, of some few years earlier, the creator's ego is on the surface suppressed and, as befits an *elogium* of Rome's rebirth, no Achilles need threaten the city's present and future calm.

Nevertheless we must remind ourselves one final time that power remains a major theme throughout the *Carmen*—the power of the Sibyl and her verses as well as of the song of the Fates, the power of the gods and of Augustus and his *Quindecimviri,* the magical potential of the young choristers and of the charming words they are given to voice. But, though the gods immerse themselves into this new Rome and though Augustus may implement what they bestow, yet not only does the poet absorb the authority of Sibyl and Fates and by his language infuse divinity into Aeneas and his posterity, he also creates that posterity and its *auctoritas.* For all the self-suppression that a public song of supplication at the *Ludi* demanded of him, Horace is very much present, as he is in all of his poems, as its creator and therefore as constructor of the Rome whose renewal it seeks. The poet fulfills the songs of Sibyl and Fates and makes the requests of Augustus come true. As the vatic chorus turns prayer into reality, its trainer's imagination brings it into being through the incantatory dynamism of poetry. His "charm" and the ritual prayer that his song outlines are one and the same.

5

Horace and the
Hellenic Heritage

We now turn to the Hellenic heritage on which Horace drew as
he composed the *Carmen*. It is Pindar who looms largest in this
background, in particular his fragmentary sixth *Paean*, which
was a principal model for *c.* 4. 6.

Pindar's *Paean* 6 has in common with *c.* 4. 6 and the *Carmen* the fact that it is addressed to Apollo and, with the *Carmen* specifically, its presentation by a chorus that speaks in the
first person singular as if it stood for Pindar himself, just as the
chorus of the *Carmen* does, and does not, serve as a surrogate for
Horace the poet. Like the *Carmen* it was publicly performed, as
part of a *theoxenia* at which the god was duly honored. And like
the *Carmen* and *c.* 4. 6, it begins with supplication of the local
divinity (in this respect, too, we have a parallel between Delphi's
imposing shrine, completed in 510, and Augustus' brilliant new
temple). But a major difference between Pindar's poem and the
Carmen soon becomes apparent. Pindar's prayer is apotropaic as
well as honorific. His hymn is meant "to ward off helplessness
from your kinsmen and from my own honors" (10-11) as song
had at an earlier time relieved Greece of famine (64-65).[1] For
Horace in the *Carmen* the stress is not on evil averted but on
good secured.

The core of the paean, and its best-preserved segment, deals
with aspects of Apollo's role in the fighting around Troy. It is
the Apollo that Horace captures well in the opening stanzas
of *c.* 4. 6—given to violence, especially to the savagery of ven-

detta. The god rages first against Achilles who, as in Horace, would have done whatever harm he could to the Trojans had not Apollo intervened. He then turns against Neoptolemus, the son of Achilles, the sacker of Troy who raises Apollo's particular ire for his murder of the aged Priam.[2]

The parallels in both content and tone between Pindar and the initial half of *c.* 4. 6 are readily apparent. Both speak to Achillean energy and to the constancy of vengeance in the god's career, whether the recipient of his anger be Niobe, Tityos, or Achilles himself before Troy. The fact that Horace chooses to imitate Pindar so closely, in a poem that not only was published a brief four years after the *Carmen* was produced but also told of that very performance, points up emphatically, again, details that the *Carmen* echoes and ones it suppresses. The violence of Achilles and the vengeance of Apollo take up half the ode. The counterbalancing segment looks to the sustaining power of the poet, his song, and the divinities he hymns. None of the content of the central section of the paean or of the opening of *c.* 4. 6 appears in the *Carmen*. Just as we now have no need for apotropaic song, so Apollo in his vengeful guise is totally absent.

The paean, however, if such is the proper sense of a corrupt text, does end positively, with mention of good health, celebration, and feasting.[3] Prayer and praise go together, as they do in the *Carmen*. The *Carmen* also reminds us that Apollo does have a weapon he has now sheathed, which is to say that he can be a god of war, but in the context of 17 B.C.E. he is a bulwark of strength and supportive of Augustan peace. It also says that the complexities of the *Aeneid* are past, that Augustus can be gentle to his fallen enemy without the disquieting implication that his foe is his brother. Thus Pindar, through the total context of *c.* 4. 6, is much in evidence as Horace praises Apollo. But the ode has a good deal to tell us both about the poet's writing, and our understanding, of the *Carmen*, as much for what the later Horatian poem demonstrates that the secular song has absorbed from Pindar as for what it excludes.[4]

The ode's Hellenic heritage from Sappho and Alcaeus must also be considered here.[5] The public presentation of the *Carmen* as choral lyric would seem to ally it most directly with Pindar's epinician odes, which were performed by a chorus either immediately after the athlete's victory or at his home city at a later time. Horace's adoption for his communal song of the meter that bears Sappho's name, the most simple that he employs in his lyrics, therefore, points up several anomalies. Horace can, when he chooses, utilize meters verging on Pindaric complexity to address divinities. The fourth Asclepiadean, for instance, is the medium for *c.* 3. 25, an ode apostrophizing Bacchus for his inspirational power. But Horace's selection of Sapphic meter for his unique public choral ode thwarts our assumptions. First, we expect Pindaric complexity of projection and do not find it. Second, the first three books of odes have schooled us to believe that, were Horace to turn to the poets of Lesbos in search of a model for oral, communal song, Alcaeus would have been his choice. After all, his most frequently used meter is designated Alcaic, and in two odes—*c.* 1. 32 and 2. 13—he singles out Alcaeus for special praise, in the latter poem to the detriment of Sappho. It is Alcaeus who, though he also sings of love's personal emotionality, is known more as the poet of the community's ordeals or, as Horace would have it, of arms and the hardships of seafaring, of exile and of war.

It is striking, therefore, that by opting for the rhythms of Sappho for the *Carmen*, Horace not only chooses a monodic rather than a choral meter in the manner of Pindar, but in particular a monodic meter associated not with the public themes of Alcaeus, who on the surface at least would appear an especially appropriate model for the Roman master, but with one of the most immediately private and personal poets of antiquity.[6]

We may speculate on the various reasons for Horace's decision. One is the meter's very facility, with three repeated Sapphic hendecasyllabic lines followed by a single Adonic. This relative simplicity would make Horace's words easy for his choristers to memorize and for the audience to comprehend on first hearing.

There are also two ways to look at the choice of Sapphic meter metaphorically. Alcaeus' poetry, as Horace describes it in précis, is centered on the politics of tyranny and on war. The content of the *Carmen*, by contrast, puts bellicosity in the past.[7] Although the chronicle of Rome from Troy to 17 B.C.E. is literally central to the ode, this very act of contextualization places her heroism in a setting where war's violence has been superseded by peace and a restored fertility. We are historically in a world beyond martial heroism just as the realm of the *Aeneid,* and the need to write epic story, is a thing of the past.[8] We are now poetically embracing not only Apollo, with his Actian bow no longer necessary, but Diana, and with Diana come chaste virgins and young child-bearing mothers as well as the local landscape of woods and mountains.[9] True *virtus,* as impetus for the saga of men, manliness, and stalwart behavior, has been crucial for Rome's development and makes a prominent appearance in the *Carmen* for the daring of her return to Augustus' Rome. But the *Carmen* embraces a whole populace, women as well as men, and views it at a universal celebration for the city's domestic well-being. It is to their homes, after all, that the chorus carries the thoughts behind their prayers once the Palatine festivity is past. For such purposes Sappho and her warmth of personal expression are entirely suitable.

We must also remember that, unlike the presentations of Sappho, Alcaeus, and Pindar, Horace's grand ode would no doubt have soon been made available to the reading public. Thus the poet's choice of meter may have had another metaphoric side to it, connoting that the poem would be perused in private as well as performed in public. It would therefore be contemplated by an ongoing series of individuals capable of appreciating in solitude, as part of an intimate, personal experience, its rich resonances.

The *Carmen* is unique in ancient poetry and in the Horatian corpus for a series of reasons. For one, it stands alone without the context of a poetry book to help give it intellectual definition. It was also read as well as heard, absorbed by means of the eye as well as registered through the ear. Nonetheless, in the circumstances of its initial, oral presentation it has close similarities to the work especially of Alcaeus and Pindar. The mere act of public performance brings with it a form of responsibility not, at least directly, attached to Horace's previous or later written work but shared with the archaic poets. On the surface, Horace here cannot propose himself as the solipsistic creator of discrete lyrics, to be studied in infinitely variable modes, not least because they are given special nuances by their contexts. On this occasion he is a public spokesman, through the chorus, for the community.

He would therefore here seem to sacrifice the subversive elements of lyric, where the special, responsive "I" stands, with egoistic particularity, confronting the demands of society and the poet's accountability toward them. As ratifier through magic song of a cultic moment of significance in a religious and political setting of the highest visibility, Horace confirms the bonds that unite a community and define its goals. For this singular moment, his gifts are at the service of Roman ideology in its larger concerns, such as the peaceful wielding of power, rather than of his own subjectivity. His words must serve as comprehensive memorial of past customs and as a reminder, for the future, of what is ethically normative and paradigmatic. He is the maker of a literal and spiritual *monumentum* for Rome and Romans, of a poem that both warns and recollects as it teaches all the while.

It is the mission of poet and poem not only to outline appropriate *mores* for the Roman community but to emphasize the idea of instruction. The youth of Rome is to be *docilis* and the chorus that sings to it *doctus*, for in important ways they are one and the same. The fifty-four singers are a synecdoche for the youth of Rome, both taught and teaching, as the outlet of a master who, in this grand instance, takes on the mantle of the archaic Greek poets as great public educators who absorb, interpret, and transmit traditional values to the population at large.[10]

When we look at the poem from this, literally, moral point of view, the idea of home, as voiced at the poem's conclusion, takes on greater puissance than I have previously allowed it. The individual poet and the separate members of the chorus are not merely pulled together into the sphere of public collectivity only to disperse once more into a number of isolated entities after the performance is over and the festival completed. Rather, just as the chorus represents the youth of the city, so the houses to which each performer in the chorus returns stand for the city as a whole. The entrance of domesticity at the end of the *Carmen* is not so much a sign of individuality restored as of public morality celebrated by stand-ins for the citizen group both transferred to, and reaffirmed in, the private nuclear household.

But, for all its parallels to the oral lyric of archaic Greece as a crucial segment of a public performance on a singular occasion for whose presentation the social consciousness of the author is fundamental, the *Carmen* was also inscribed, and presumably published, shortly after the conclusion of the festival it graced. Thus, though it shares with Alcaeus and Pindar the notion of poetry as a vital part of the communal enterprise, the ready opportunity open to Horace's Roman public for perusal of the written text would also bring, in a way not immediately available to the audiences of the archaic Greek poets, a chance forthwith to explore the poet's own creative, imaginative, subjective self, especially through contemplation of his allusions. Horace's brilliance, which finds its outlet not least in figures of sound and sense, in imagery, in the play of rhythm and the balance of structure, only offers further affirmation of the validity of the *Carmen* as an educational device.[11]

Let us pause for one further moment specifically on Pindar, especially given the fact that Horace's *Carmen* and Pindar's best-preserved masterpieces, the epinician odes, are choral songs intended for public performance before a specific audience.[12] Both poets are bringers of praise, Horace of Rome and Augustus, Pindar of his athletic victors and of the glory that accrues through them to family, to patron and trainer, and to native cities. Pindar regularly uses myth to enhance his odes, more often than not by comparing present to past in order to highlight the victor's accomplishment by analogy with earlier examples of heroism or, on occasion, to differentiate between then and now. So too Horace, at the center of his poem, elaborates the myth of Aeneas in order to draw parallels between the founder of Rome and the physical and metaphysical accomplishment of his journey of establishment and Augustus, Rome's literal and spiritual renewer. Just as Pindar's athletic heroes form individual segments in a pan-Hellenism held together by language, religion, and a common mythic heritage, so Aeneas, Romulus, and Augustus are but prominent names in a universal continuum we call Rome, whose victorious progress is as much the result of ethical and moral achievements as of the broad acquisition of political and military power.

But the differences between the poets also deserve recognition. We can start with poetic arrangement itself. Pindar's odes are regularly triadic in structure, dealing first with the victor and the diverse meanings of his deed, then in the central third, with myth and its complementary roles, and finally, at the end, with the victor once again and the ramifications of his heroism. There are elements of a similar ring-composition in Horace as well, with the beginning of his ode echoed in its conclusion and with the story of Aeneas appropriately entering the poem at its center. But Horace's ode is carefully cumulative as well as cyclical. It bends back on itself but it is also built of halves piled on each other so that the circle and the line form for the reader a creative friction with each other.

The circle and the line are also powerfully metaphoric for the poem itself. The circle dramatizes that history repeats itself, that, in this case, Rome is capable of inner and outer renewal and refreshment, whether these be gained through a chain of individual accomplishments that meld into a whole or by the repetition of celebrations of the *saeculum* and the new beginnings that they, too, postulate. The line proposes that history, at least Roman history, also has a strong teleological element about it that leads developmentally to its pinnacle of greatness under Augustus and to a proclamation of that greatness on a particular spot at a specially designated hour on a June day of 17 B.C.E..

This very linearity marks what is certainly one of the major differences between Horace and his Greek predecessor. Pindar regularly makes us aware of the passage of time, most readily perhaps in the temporal differentiations his appeal to myth engenders and in his acknowledgment that poetry and its repeated performances can bring immortality to its subjects. He is also cognizant of the topographical and geographical diversity that make up the Greek world whence his victors spring. This said, we can only marvel at the deepened intensity with which, by comparison, Horace in the *Carmen* approaches the categories of time and space. As far as the latter is concerned, in the course of this single poem we stretch our vision from a particular spot on the Palatine in front of a temple of whose details we take note, to the city with its seven hills, below and beyond, to Latium and its eastern mountain border and, finally, to the distant boundaries of empire where the city's enemies cower before the martial dynamism that emanates from Alban Rome.

As for time, we might look again at Horace's appropriation of the Aeneas legend and compare it with Pindar's use of myth. For both poets, myth serves to create metaphor by analogy, offering to the listener/reader the opportunity to reimagine from a variety of angles of vision the present in relation to the past. But Horace offers something more, for Aeneas is at once part of myth and part of history.[13] The history of Rome, which is to say history in both its expansiveness and in its compendious particularity, begins with the hero's departure from the flames of Troy for the Etruscan shore. And, if we look at the heroes who people Rome's world, it begins with Aeneas and leads in a continuum, that is also climactic, to Augustus, whose deeds form the acme of a millennium of events of which the Romans and their poets, unlike the lyric geniuses of archaic Greece, were keenly conscious.

6

The *Carmen Saeculare*
and Latin Poetry

The influence of Horace's Roman poetic heritage, in particular the work of Catullus, Virgil, and Tibullus, is also apparent in the *Carmen*. In my discussion I will follow this order chronologically.

The most salient example of Catullus' presence in Horace's ode is as obvious as the work itself is anomalous within the earlier poet's corpus, namely, poem 34, his hymn to Diana:

> Dianae sumus in fide
> puellae et pueri integri:
> [Dianam pueri integri]
>   puellaeque canamus.
>
> o Latonia, maximi
> magna progenies Iovis,
> quam mater prope Deliam
>   deposivit olivam,
>
> montium domina ut fores
> silvarumque virentium
> saltuumque reconditorum
>   amniumque sonantum:
>
> tu Lucina dolentibus
> Iuno dicta puerperis,
> tu potens Trivia et notho es
>   dicta lumine Luna.

tu cursu, dea, menstruo
metiens iter annuum,
rustica agricolae bonis
      tecta frugibus exples.

sis quocumque tibi placet
sancta nomine, Romulique,
antique ut solita es, bona
      sospites ope gentem.

We girls and chaste boys are in the service of Diana:
we, [chaste boys] and girls hymn [Diana]. O daughter of Latona, mighty offspring of mightiest Jupiter,
whom your mother bore beside the olive of Delos,
that you might be mistress of mountains and green
woods and hidden glens and sounding streams: you
are called Juno the Light-Bringer by women in the
pangs of childbirth, you are called mighty Trivia and
Moon with borrowed light. Goddess, measuring the
path of the year by your monthly course, you fill the
rustic dwelling of the farmer with produce. Be you
worshipped by whatever name pleases, and, as has
been your wont of old, may you keep safe the race
of Romulus with good resource.

    We know nothing of the occasion of the poem's presentation,[1]
but, unlike the hymns of Horace's initial collection of odes, it
shares with the *Carmen* many of the hallmarks of public performance, as if Horace in 17 skipped over his own earlier writing and returned for inspiration to the unmediated directness of
his great predecessor's work. In general terms, one major difference between the works is the tone and rhetoric of each ending.
Catullus, following the tradition of hymns, ends his poem with
the second-person invocation and prayer that he had adopted

throughout, complete with the escape clause *quocumque nomine* ("by whatever name") in case his apostrophes and their concomitant attributes be found wanting in the eyes of the goddess.[2] Horace drops such prominent features of hymnic procedure in his poem's concluding six stanzas as with blatant brilliance he presumes the efficacy of his words. Nevertheless at the start of their respective poems both poets immerse us forthwith in the chorus and its song, Catullus through *sumus* (1) and *canamus* (9), Horace by means of *precamur* (3). It is natural also that because Catullus' hymn is oriented strictly toward Diana, it is in the segments of the *Carmen* devoted to the goddess that we might expect the impact of poem 34 to be most closely felt. Horace's initial *silvarumque potens* and later mentions of Aventinus and Algidus remind us of Catullus' address to Diana as mistress of mountains "and of greening woods" (*silvarumque virentium*, 11), and his references to Diana as Lucina and Luna follow Catullus' example (13-16).

But there is also a larger rhythm to Catullus with which Horace empathizes. Catullus shifts from Diana as goddess of the wilds to presider over childbirth and, as lunar, monthly emblem (*cursu menstruo*, 18) of the year's path (*iter annuum*, 19) over the fertility of the agricultural world. The poem ends with an entrance into Roman historical specifics as the chorus prays that Diana keep safe (*sospites*, 24) with good resource the race of Romulus (*Romuli ... gentem*, 22-24). We move, in other words, from Diana as goddess of the wild, first to human begetting, then to agricultural, georgic nature and, finally, to the actual Romans, those born of Romulus, who people the land.

This intellectual progress is not unlike that of Horace who begins with Diana as divinity of woods and turns shortly to her role as goddess of parturition. Then, after he has formulated the change from Troy to Rome, Horace subsumes Diana into the repeated *di* of his final apostrophe as his chorus prays for the continued prosperity of Romulus' race (*Romulae genti*). Just as Catullus passes from childbirth to yearly time to historical chronology by way of the mention of Romulus, so Horace likewise moves from childbearing to the fertility of the land to the well-being of Romulus' descendants.[3] His figure of transition is Aeneas, and it is to him that Horace allots the greatest concentration of lexical parallels with Catullus (*sospite cursu, iter*). Diana's yearly course forms in the earlier poem a movement parallel to Aeneas' voyage in Horace's ode. Literally this takes us from Troy to Rome, but in terms of Horace's poetic journey, we proceed through the passage of mortal time, of the sun's daily round, of human nativity, of the earth's fullness, to historical temporality. Aeneas, therefore, through verbal usage and through his role in the modulation of the poem, claims resemblance to Catullus' Diana. The resulting compliment is clear enough.

The second poem of Catullus that broods over the *Carmen Saeculare* is his masterpiece, poem 64. Here the intellectual influence is more general than specific but its current runs deeply. At only one moment does Horace precisely betray his attention to Catullus' great poem. In the seventh stanza of the *Carmen* Horace draws the Fates into his poem, the "Parcae truthful in your song" (*veraces cecinisse Parcae*, 25). He reminds us thereby of the concluding episode of Catullus' poem and of how

> veridicos Parcae coeperunt edere cantus.[4]

> the Parcae began to give utterance to their truth-telling song.

Soon thereafter the narrator reaffirms the veracity of their pronouncement:

> talia divino fuderunt carmine fata,
> carmine, perfidiae quod post nulla arguet aetas.[5]

> [The Fates] poured forth the following prophecy in
> divine song, song which no future age will accuse of
> untruth.

In the subsequent words of the Parcae themselves, they are voic-
ing a "truth-telling oracle" (*veridicum oraclum*, 326).

The veracity of the Fates' song is what Horace asks us to remember from Catullus, but in so doing he also expects us to
recall the contents of the song itself and its ideological setting.
This in turn invites us to compare and contrast Catullus' view
of the evolution of human history with the vision of contemporary Rome that Horace's new song has the Fates shore up with
their supportive chant. Catullus 64 looks at two virtually contemporaneous events—the launching and voyage of the *Argo,*
man's initial sea journey, and the resulting nuptials of Peleus and
Thetis. It is at the marriage ceremony, the central subject of the
poem, that the Fates sing their ritual song.

But, like the ambiguous consequences of the *Argo*'s intrigues
and of marine adventuring in general, the wedding was also a
pivotal moment in myth. It served as the last occasion when
gods and mortals mingled together. Moreover the offspring of
the union between goddess and mortal was Achilles whose bru-
tal virtuosity is at the core of the Fates' epithalamium. Catullus'
ironic view of heroism looks both before and after within the
poem. It serves as commentary on the lengthy ekphrasis describing the coverlet on the couple's bridal couch, which detailed the
desertion of Ariadne by Theseus, a further illustration of a hero's
less-than-exemplary behavior. It also anticipates the poem's epi-
logue, which constitutes a diatribe on the difference between a
more moral past, when immortals shared in the lives of humankind, and the present, when the evil ways of men keep the gods
apart.

One further detail leads us back to the *Carmen.* All the gods, so the narrator tells us, attend the wedding of Peleus and Thetis save Apollo and Diana. No reason is given within the poem for this enigmatic absence, but both the context of poem 64 and the reaction to it in the *Carmen* may suggest an answer. The twin divinities are unable to bear witness to the advent of an age where heroism goes awry, where seafaring augments the greed of man's ambitions and the warriors at Troy, whose chief glory is Achilles in all his pitiless savagery, forecast present human decadence. The renewed presences of Diana and Apollo in human affairs are central, not to say crucial, in the ode. Horace's enchanting song, unlike the riveting but bitter hymn of the Fates in Catullus 64, can once again co-opt divinity into showing active concern for mankind. His magical ode gives assurance of the dynamic presence of the sacred in our profane existences.

But this return to an age of divine sustenance of our mortal lot, as Catullus richly implies, will only materialize through a renaissance of quality in human morality. In the case of Horace's contemporary Rome it can occur only when the focal heroic figure is not given to barbaric violence but instead is an Augustus, Rome's holy aggrandizer, the new Aeneas who has again passed through the cleansing of Troy's fire so as to bring about a time when sacred and profane, divine and human, can again commingle as mankind renews its ethical values and, through the medium of Horace's incantatory verse, the gods, especially now Apollo and Diana, hear and respond to the emperor's salutary requests as they share in his ceremony.

Another masterpiece written some fifteen years after Catullus' is Virgil's *eclogue* 4, whose dramatic date is 40 B.C.E., the year of the consulship of its dedicatee, Asinius Pollio. It serves as an effective intellectual bridge between Catullus 64 and the *Carmen*. The connection with the latter is already clear from lines 4–5 of the *eclogue:*

> Ultima Cumaei venit iam carminis aetas;
> magnus ab integro saeclorum nascitur ordo.

> Now the last age of Cumaean song has come. The
> great line of the ages is born anew.

First we have the formative adjacency of *carminis* and *saeclorum*. Then we listen to the language of the Sibyl, *Cumaei . . . carminis,* incorporated into the texture of Horace's poem as *Sibyllini versus.* Reference to the *saecula* recurs later in the poem with the appearance of the Fates (46–47):

> "Talia saecula" suis dixerunt "currite" fusis
> concordes stabili fatorum numine Parcae.

> "Ages such as this, run on," the Fates cried to their
> spindles, agreeing on the unchanging will of destiny.

Since Virgil is looking directly back to the refrain Catullus gives to the Fates in his sixty-fourth poem, Horace in one stanza bows to the first two of his major Latin influences (25–28):

> Vosque, veraces cecinisse Parcae,
> quod semel dictum est stabilisque rerum
> terminus servet, bona iam peractis
>   iungite fata.

This time, absorbing the language of the Fates as complement to that of the Sibyl into his own larger act of genius, Horace comes still closer to echoing the earlier poem of his friend. Iteration of Parcae and of forms of *dicere* and *fata* directly suggest the allusion that is confirmed by the echo of *stabili numine* in *stabilis . . . terminus.*

    Another salient reminiscence of *eclogue* 4 in the *Carmen* remarked on by commentators is the triple use of *iam* in anaphora at 53–57, beholden to the three uses of *iam* at *ecl.* 4. 5–10, the first two likewise in anaphora.[6] The line begun by Virgil's initial *iam*[7]—

> iam redit et virgo redeunt Saturnia regna . . .

> Now the Virgin returns, now the kingdom of Saturn returns.

—stands out in particular for its relation to *Carmen Saeculare* 57–59:

> iam Fides et Pax et Honos Pudorque
> priscus et neglecta redire Virtus
> audet . . .

Horace alters Virgil's *Iustitia* (the virgin *Dike*, as she appears earlier in Aratus) to *Virtus*,[8] and the pastoral poet's open mention of the advent of a new *gens aurea*, a golden race, is limited by the indirection of the odist's reference to Copia and her lavish horn. Nevertheless, renewal is a focal notion of each poem. It is embodied for Virgil in the larger myth of the ages of men, restored in the poet's imagination to a golden new beginning. For Horace it more strictly entails the Roman idea of a prescribed, ritually oriented *saeculum*, which brings with it not so much an imagined, idealized Saturnian dream of peace and plenty as the restoration of allegiance to an ancient and pristine—yet realistic—form of *Virtus* and to nature's fresh postbellum plenitude paralleling mankind's revived uprightness of spirit.

Additional lexical overlaps further the continuum between the two poems. Among these one goes without saying: the constant presence in each of singing and song. There is a common emphasis on birth and offspring.[9] The notion of temporality permeates both eclogue and ode in a variety of ways.[10] Diana as Lucina appears in apostrophe in both poems, in the fourth *eclogue* accompanied immediately by "your Apollo" (*tuus*

Apollo).[11] Both works speak of *decus* at important moments and in each the fertility of earth is a prominent theme.[12]

But, for all the conspicuous parallels between the two poems, it is as if Horace were referring to Virgil's brilliant achievement to illustrate how his own poem and his further reinvention of Rome have superseded the pastoral poet's gripping vision while carefully building upon it. During the year of the poem's dramatic date a further reconciliation was attempted between Octavian, Antony, and their factions, but it was also during the winter of 41–40 that the former's soon notorious acts of brutality against the citizens of Perusia took place. Since the temper of the times was at best unsettled, Virgil's extraordinary leap of imagination stems more from whimsical hope than from any real prospect of a speedy return to, or revival of, some halcyon era. And, although in *eclogue* 4 all menace seems to evaporate from an all-productive nature at the birth of the boy on whom the poem centers, nevertheless his life span will see a new *Argo* and a new Achilles before—so the poet fancies—a settled time of universal plenitude will recur:[13]

> alter erit tum Tiphys et altera quae vehat Argo
> delectos heroas; erunt etiam altera bella
> atque iterum ad Troiam magnus mittetur Achilles.

> Then there will be another Tiphys and another Argo
> to carry chosen heroes. There will also be other wars
> and again mighty Achilles will be sent to Troy.

Virgil carefully reminds us of where we saw this poetic series begin, with Catullus 64 and the shallow, violent heroism of which it tells, brought on by the *Argo*'s voyage and culminating in the barbarism of Achilles. Only when this has been reexperienced and, as it were, purged will nature spontaneously beget what man in his ambition had previously sought through force of arms. Everything is couched in a future time that only becomes present in the *Carmen Saeculare*. And it is appropriate that Horace, as he celebrates such a moment, purge both *Argo* and Achilles from his poetry even as he bows respectfully toward their potent appearances in the poetry of the recent past. The appetitiveness for which the *Argo* stands and Achillean violence can have no part in the new Augustan dispensation.

Horace in the *Carmen* not only reaches back to a time when gods cared for men but imagines into present actuality a world that for Virgil remains only a flight of fancy. There has indeed been another siege of Roman immorality, in the climax of a century of civil war, but the boy has now grown to manhood and in very fact metamorphosed into Augustus. Virgil's imagined birth of a child has been realized by Horace as the rebirth of Rome with Augustus grown into full *auctoritas*, with war behind him and an immediate prospect of a new beginning for man and nature. Achilles is at least here obliterated from poetic memory as Apollo and Diana, in the extraordinary "indicativeness" of the *Carmen*'s incantatory conclusion, again share in fostering the activities of humanity.[14]

The language of *eclogue* 4 suffuses the *Carmen* but is most prominent on two occasions, in the stanza addressed to the Fates and their song and in the verses that follow on Horace's description of Augustus' prayer. Horace assimilates and reprojects each voice through the potency of his own words, thereby both confirming the stability of Rome's destiny and reasserting the emperor's wishes to the gods. In so doing he affirms and authorizes in particular two aspects of Virgil's earlier vision, namely, that the Fates' song has in fact come true and that Apollo along with his sister does indeed reign again in a Rome very much part of a historical "now."

Virgil of the *Aeneid* is also a strong presence throughout the *Carmen*. The central stanza, in particular, resonates with echoes of the recently published poem as it initiates a sequence from Troy to Rome, beginning with *castus* Aeneas, leading to the chorus' imprecation that Roman youth practice *probros mores*, and thence to Augustus' own time of prayer and its dramatic outcome as the poem scans its results in the immediate world of Rome. The allusion to *Aeneid* 6 in lines 49–52 is especially provocative. Not only do Augustus and Aeneas merge as a result of the suggestive reference to Anchises and Venus, but Horace, through his singers, by transmuting his words actually adopts the persona of Anchises as he addresses his son in the underworld and calls him *Romane*, incorporation of Rome, and therefore of Augustus, to come.[15] He is creating, or better re-creating, the emperor as his own spiritual child. In so doing he has a particular purpose that directly anticipates the remainder of the poem and the palpability of Rome's regeneration. In importuning Aeneas to remember, as he puts his *virtus* into practice, "to spare the subjected and to subdue the proud through war" (*parcere subiectis et debellare superbos*), Anchises urges a mode of future conduct that Aeneas in the last books of the epic and most prominently in the violence of its concluding climax is unwilling or unable to follow.[16]

Father Anchises is asking his gradually empowered son to become habituated to an ethical use of power that he, and by extension Rome, seem yet incapable of implementing. Horace's art again turns Virgil's future into Rome's present, hope into truth, idealized Aeneas into realized Augustus. Virgil's Aeneas, who in victory ought, according to his father, to spare his defeated foe but does not, has modulated into the hero's reincarnation as an Augustus who is in fact "superior to his warring [foe], gentle to the fallen enemy" (*bellante prior, iacentem / lenis in hostem*). Anchises' role as educator to future Rome has passed to Horace as singer of her present quality. Through the poet's charm, as prayer passes into fact for the final third of the ode,

Apollo has indeed returned his arrows to their quiver, and his terrestrial counterpart has learned to put into effect the combination of strength and moderation that for both Virgil and Horace typifies Rome's mission at its most civilized.

The last of the major influences on Horace as he wrote the *Carmen* is the fifth elegy of Tibullus' second book.[17] The longest and most "Roman" of Tibullus' poems, it concerns the induction of Messalinus, son of the elegist's patron, M. Valerius Messalla Corvinus, into the ranks of the *Quindecimviri sacris faciundis* who were the overseers of the Sibylline books and who figure prominently in line 70 of the *Carmen* as priests to whose prayers (*preces*) Diana responds. Their voices in Horace's poem join those of the chorus (*precamur*) and of the other "languages" of the poem and add a notable religious dimension to them. Since in the inscription of the *Acta* the name of Messalinus is placed last in the list of members of the priesthood in attendance, we can assume that his inauguration was recent. Moreover, because the ancient evidence puts the death of Tibullus as contemporary with that of Virgil, that is, in 19 B.C.E., it is likely that the elegy was written not long before that date, with publication soon afterwards.[18] It was therefore given to the public at roughly the same time as the *Aeneid,* that is to say some two or three years before the *Ludi* were held.

Even if we look only at superficial details, the parallels between the two poems are striking. The first word in each poem is an apostrophe to Apollo as Phoebus:

> Phoebe, fave! novus ingreditur tua templa sacerdos:
> huc age cum cithara carminibusque veni.

> Phoebus, look with favor! A new priests enters your temple. Make your way hither with lyre and songs.

The poem ends as it began, with Phoebus now joined by his unnamed sister, so that Diana enters the poem to have the last word (121–22):

> adnue! sic tibi sint intonsi, Phoebe, capilli,
> > sic tua perpetuo sit tibi casta soror.

> Nod approval! Thus may your locks remain unshorn, thus may your sister remain forever chaste.

Meanwhile we find ourselves in the same setting as that of the *Carmen,* on the Palatine before the temple (*templa*) of Apollo, this time with the single voice of the poet-speaker—rather than with a plurality of choristers—enouncing the appropriate prayer (*precor,* 4).[19] The god is visualized in postwar, that is post-Actian, guise, bright and beautiful,[20] his hair kempt once more, looking as he did, says the speaker, when he sang the praises of Jupiter after Saturn had been exiled. We behold the god of music and song, but we soon turn to Apollo as god of prophecy,[21] in particular as patron-inspirer of the Sibyl,[22] and then to the seeress herself (19–22):

> haec dedit Aeneae sortes, postquam ille parentem
> > dicitur et raptos sustinuisse Lares:
> (nec fore credebat Romam, cum maestus ab alto
> > Ilion ardentes respiceretque deos . . .).

> She gave predictions to Aeneas after he is said to have lifted up his father and the Lares he had snatched (nor did he believe that there would be a Rome when in sadness he beheld from the deep Ilium and its burning shrines).

After a brief digression on the simplicity of life in what was then Rome, Tibullus returns to the Sibyl and to twenty-six lines of her imagined prophecy to Aeneas, beginning (39–42):

"impiger Aenea, volitantis frater Amoris,
      Troica qui profugis sacra vehis ratibus,
iam tibi Laurentes adsignat Iuppiter agros,
      iam vocat errantes hospita terra Lares."

"Eager Aeneas, brother of winged Love, who carry
Troy's holy objects on your ships of exile, now Jupiter assigns you the Laurentian fields, now a welcom-
ing land calls your wandering Lares."

Not only does the language smack of Virgil, it also anticipates
in theme and execution the focal stanzas of the *Carmen* where
we have Ilian throngs commencing the journey to Italy, Lares
forced to change their abodes, and an Aeneas who makes his
way without hurt from burning Troy (*ardentem Troiam*).

    The Sibyl's prophecy then takes us from the defeat of Tur-
nus to the rape of Ilia and to a still more distant future where
Ceres looks down from heaven on "her fields," which now means
the whole world, with Rome ruling east and west alike. When
her speech is finished, Tibullus proceeds explicitly to name four
sibyls, as if to lend force to what follows—eight powerful lines
detailing the prodigies and portents that occurred subsequent
to the death of Julius Caesar.[23] These range from comets and
a rain of stones to arms resounding in the heavens, an eclipse
of the sun, weeping statues, and talking cattle. Such manifestations, too, like the warring they anticipated, are things of the
past (79–80):

haec fuerant olim; sed tu iam mitis, Apollo,
      prodigia indomitis merge sub aequoribus.

These things were once-upon-a-time; but, Apollo,
now gentle, sink the prodigies beneath untamed
waters.

Here, too, we think explicitly of the *Carmen* and of the later poet's parallel command to the same god (33–34):

> condito mitis placidusque telo
> supplices audi pueros, Apollo; . . .

And so with good omens we can observe the Roman present, with Ceres bursting her barns with grain, with the drunken farmer leaping through flames during the celebration of the Palilia,[24] with feasting and love-making.[25] The poet may be unhappy with Nemesis unresponsive to his song, but this does not keep him from envisioning Messalinus in triumph or from concluding with the final prayer to Apollo and his sister.

The overlap between the two poems is evident, beginning with the clear parallels in setting and ceremony. Apollo is the primary addressee of Tibullus as he is prominent in the *Carmen*. The story of Aeneas plays a crucial role in each poem, and the Sibyl figures also, more in the foreground for Tibullus, in the background in Horace's treatment. But there are also many differences between the two poems that will help us elucidate aspects of the odist's originality. One obvious distinction is the mode of performance. Horace's song was delivered orally as the concluding offering of an extraordinary three-day public ritual. It fosters the illusion of an unmediated prayer by innocent young singers, with the ego of the creative poet suppressed. In Tibullus' poem, although Apollo is apostrophized at its beginning and end and although we are meant to visualize the god's new priest entering the Palatine temple, we are nevertheless reading an imagined account of a ceremony with a series of elegiac embellishments, not hearing the voices of actual performers. Tibullus asks his god to come to the proceedings "with lyre and songs" (*carminibus*). Horace offers a *carmen* itself. There is no prayer for inspiration, only the inspired, immediate song. Prayer is directed toward other ends.

Then there are crucial variations in the way each poet treats the god himself. Tibullus' Apollo has his temples crowned with the laurel of a triumphator (*triumphali devinctus tempora lauro*, 5), and we have already seen in the potential allegory of Jupiter besting Saturn that the elegist would have us ponder Apollo's role at the decisive battle when Octavian defeated Antony. Horace's poem leaves negative aspects of Apollo's life in his capacity of lord of the bow, be they connected with disease or with military prowess, to the single phrases *condito telo* and *fulgente decorus arcu*.

The same distinction between the two poems holds true on a larger scale when we examine their treatments of Roman history. Tibullus, in the course of his elegy, touches on several of the more violent moments of the Roman past. At 24, by calling attention to the walls (*moenia*) of Rome, "not to be dwelt within by his confrere Remus" (*consorti non habitanda Remo*), he reminds us of Romulus' killing of his brother and its analogical consequences for the century of fratricidal strife that preceded Actium. The verses that Tibullus gives the Sibyl take us through Aeneas' killing of Turnus and the rape of Ilia by Mars on their way to present Roman greatness, and the list of portents that the sibyls as a group are said to have foretold would have recalled to the mind of every Roman reader the murder of Julius Caesar on the Ides of March, 44 B.C.E. Horace omits all such references to negative aspects of Rome's developing power. We leap from Aeneas directly to Augustus, with only a brief mention of Romulus, and intimations of allegory link the two as we turn from the founding father's journey of *castitas* and *libertas* to the *lenitas* of Rome's present renewer whose enemies sue for peace.

A further word on the Sibyl. Tibullus imagines the Sibyl directly predicting to Aeneas the future of Rome — the same situation in which Virgil had placed the Cumaean Sibyl in *Aeneid* 6 —

and then, in indirect speech, predicting the monstrous events that surrounded the death of Caesar. Horace, by contrast, becomes a type of Sibyl. He does not see what is to come, adumbrate the *prodigia* that must be suffered to be surmounted, or foretell wars to be experienced in the near or distant future. Rather Sibylline Horace, through the chorus, announces the past in his own voice, prays to the gods on behalf of the race of Romulus, asks that Augustus' requests be granted, and then pronounces their fulfillment in Rome of the present. The Sibylline books may demand the performance of *Ludi*, but Horace himself replaces the Sibyl not as prophet of the future but as reassurer of the present and of the blessings of the gods that are showered upon it. The absence of portents in any form from the *Carmen* is one of Horace's major departures from tradition, poetic or otherwise.

7

The *Carmen Saeculare* and *Carmina*

To conclude my discussion of Horace's *Carmen,* I will examine more specifically the word *carmen* and especially the situations where *carmina* were sung as part of ritual ceremonies in an attempt to determine the originality of the *Carmen Saeculare.* I will look first at the meaning and usage of the word itself and then examine the connection between *carmen/carmina* and poetic genre. Finally, I will review the history of public performance of *carmina* and, in particular, their connection with Augustus' *Ludi.*

Horace's last reference to the *Carmen* comes in what was certainly among his final works, the great letter to the emperor, *epi.* 2. 1, dated to 12 or shortly thereafter.[1] It forms an understated segment of a litany devoted to a poet's virtues. He teaches children, corrects unseemly conduct with wise precepts, educates through noble examples:[2]

> castis cum pueris ignara puella mariti
> disceret unde preces, vatem ni Musa dedisset?
> poscit opem chorus et praesentia numina sentit,
> caelestis inplorat aquas docta prece blandus,
> avertit morbos, metuenda pericula pellit,
> impetrat et pacem et locupletem frugibus annum:

> Whence would the unwedded girl, together with chaste boys, learn prayers had not the Muse given them a bard? Their chorus asks for aid and responds

to the presence of the divine, ingratiatingly with learned prayer it beseeches the gods for water, it turns aside diseases, repulses fearful dangers, gains both peace and a year rich with crops.

In the first two lines Horace refers to the preparations and performance of the *Carmen* as the muse inspires the bard who in turn instructs his young charges in the prayers they are to sing. The next lines look to the ode's contents. The phrase *praesentia numina sentit,* for instance, is a nod to the conclusion of the *Carmen* where the chorus carries away assurance that "Jupiter and all the gods respond to these [prayers]" (*Haec Iovem sentire deosque cunctos*), that is, to the combination of prayer and declaration that constitutes the poem.[3] The word *aquas* looks back to the *aquae salubres* (*C. S.* 31) that Jupiter will supply, and *frugibus* is a bow to Tellus' depiction in the *Carmen* as *fertilis frugum* (29). The verb *impetro* that Horace here assigns to the chorus is, in the *Carmen,* allotted by the chorus to Augustus as they request that he may gain what he desires (*impetret,* 51, the last use of the subjunctive in the poem).

Only line 136 lacks a parallel with the *Carmen* and in fact stands out because it brings to the fore the apotropaic potential of song, which was part of Horace's inheritance but which he chose largely to suppress in his public performance. However much *carmina* may have been used in the Roman past as a means to avert disease or ward off calamity, this negative aspect of song as charm would sound a jarring note in the essentially positive tonality of the ode. It is only hinted at in the line that rounds off this segment of the epistle (138):

> carmine di superi placantur, carmine Manes.

> The gods above are won over by song, by song the gods below.

The chorus may succeed in its desires, but this transpires only because of the poet and his *carmen*. The boys and girls are merely a suitable means of presenting the poet's enchanting words, which serve as the true artistic mediators between gods and men. Only Horace's choral song can fully exercise the power of poetry's ritual.

The etymology of *carmen* links it closely with the root *can-, to sing.[4] By the time the word first appears in recorded Latin, in the Laws of the Twelve Tables, the connection is already clear. In the eighth table we are dealing with those who put singing and song to use for purposes of evil. Pliny the Elder quotes an excerpt from the Table dealing with someone "who might have chanted an evil song" (*qui malum carmen incantassit*), and the notion is elaborated in a quotation that St. Augustine draws from Cicero's *De re publica:* "if anyone were to 'sing at' [a person] or to perform a song which would slander or incriminate another" (*si quis occentavisset sive carmen condidisset, quod infamiam faceret flagitiumve alteri . . .*).[5] And in the same context we hear of those who might be brought to justice for using "song" to lure someone else's crops, presumably into their own possession.[6] We thus find in our earliest exampled uses of *cano* and *carmen* a close association of the latter with magic and incantation, with the utterance of spells through the medium of song.

In the Twelve Tables such utterances had evil intentions that should be prohibited by law. By contrast, we find in Cato the Elder a *carmen* used for a positive purpose at the annual lustration of the fields, to ward off adverse forces so that the land will be fruitful. In both instances we are dealing not with poetry per se, that is, with language structured by meter into verse, but simply with words that if articulated properly according to due formulas can bring about a physical reaction that reifies the speaker's wishes. This response may be either positive or negative but whatever the situation, it is the result of language chanted in prayer, of words used with ritual precision so that their spell will be quite literally effective. Nevertheless, it is well to point out forthwith that the fragments we possess of early hymns, the shorter remnants of the hymn of the Salic priests and the more extensive remains of the song of the Fratres Arvales, are not only powerfully rhythmical but in verse as well.[7] Thus, though in its origin the word *carmen* demands only an association with song or incantation, in its earliest history verse is also in notable instances a strong presence in its make-up. Verse adds to the formular language of ritual prose a further dimension of ordered repetition and of schematic exactitude that allows poetic *carmina* to assume an aura of special potency.

By the end of the second century B.C.E. the word *carmen* has largely taken on the meaning "poetry," but throughout the history of Latin letters the noun's original sense of a verbal utterance sung for ritualistic purposes, of a magic spell that the proper articulation of words can cast, is never far beneath the surface of a large number of usages. We think, for instance, of the appearances, seventeen in fact, of the word *carmen* in the eighth *eclogue* of Virgil. We can contemplate the whole poem as one extensive "song" embracing two smaller magic "songs," each with repeated, intercalary lines, one of which fails in its purpose while the other "works." It is in the successful incantation that the word *carmen* most prominently appears. We find it first in the witch's pronouncement that only *carmina* are lacking to her sorcery and in her listing of the practical results of its proper utterance (drawing down of the moon, Circean transformations, bursting of snakes). But it permeates the poem most conspicuously in a line that is repeated ten times (the last in a variation) by the witch as she sings:

ducite ab urbe domum, mea carmina, ducite Daphnim.

lead home from the city, my songs, lead home
Daphnis.

The line stands out for many reasons, not least because Virgil,
in making obeisance to his model, the second *Idyl* of Theoc-
ritus, has in his repeated line replaced the latter's iunx wheel
with *carmina*. The practical, tangible tools of magic have, in
Virgil's hands, become the sung words to which the sorcer-
ess gives voice. And although her verses are delivered in dac-
tylic hexameter lines of extraordinary power, their connection
with the essential meaning of *carmen* as magic song is strongly
felt.

The same double meaning holds true of the word *carmen* in
the subsequent *eclogue*. Lycidas, walking toward the city, meets
Moeris who laments the confiscation of their fields by Rome.
Lycidas replies that he had heard that the land had been preserved by Menalcas, that

omnia carminibus vestrum servasse Menalcan.

your Menalcas had saved all with his songs.

Moeris' riposte is that "our songs" (*carmina nostra*) have as much
power against the weapons of Mars as doves do against an eagle.[8]
In both instances, again, *carmina* may signify songs in poetry just
as Menalcas may to some degree stand for Virgil, the potentially
redeeming poet to whom Rome may give ear. But likewise in
both cases the magic potential of song is explicit in the connotation of *carmina*. Whether or not it will be efficacious is another
matter.

At lines 32–34 of the ninth *eclogue* Virgil puts verses into the
mouth of Lycidas that add a further dimension to our discussion:

    ... et me fecere poetam

    Pierides, sunt et mihi carmina, me quoque dicunt

    vatem pastores; ...

    The maidens of Pieria made even me a poet. I, too,

    have songs. The shepherds also call me a bard.

The poet here calls attention to his words in several ways. The first is the punning connection between *fecere* and *poetam*, forged by means of Greek "making" become Latin and therefore the concomitant emphasis on inspiration supplied to the Roman poet by the Greek Muses. We are for a brisk moment suddenly immersed in the deeply literary world of Virgil's poetic tradition. But Lycidas is also labeled "bard" (*vatis*) by his fellow shepherds. The word is the earliest Latin word for poet.[9] It has no direct associations with Greek, and by linking it with the thinking of shepherds, Virgil allows it to take on associations not only with the unsophisticated and illiterate but also with the primitive affiliations of bards with voyeuristic behavior. They are seers, viewers into the dark, as well as entertainers through song.

    Caught in between and sharing in both spiritual realms are Lycidas' *carmina*. As poetic songs they are the (present) culmination of a long literary tradition of brilliant verse production from Homer to Virgil. In association with the speaker as bard and soothsayer, they also smack of the elemental power of song to charm and of singers to exert a power beyond the ordinary through their minstrelsy.

    Both meanings remain attached to mentions of *carmina* throughout Augustan poetry. Here it is instructive to remember what contexts Horace gives to himself as "maker" of the *Carmen Saeculare*. The first is at the end of *c.* 4. 6 where the former chorister, now bride, can claim

> reddidi carmen docilis modorum
>   vatis Horati.

> I, instructed in the modes of the bard Horace, ren-
> dered the song.

The phrase *vatis Horati* can, in the Latin, serve to modify either *carmen* or *modi*. Both the song and its measures are associated with Horace, and Horace gives himself, at the conclusion of his poem outlining the genesis of the *Carmen,* the designation *vatis,* Latin, not Greek, word for song-maker.[10] Likewise, in his epistle to Augustus, we recall, preceding a summary view of the power of song (*carmen*) to please the gods of both heaven and under-world, "Horace" tells his emperor that there would be no one to instruct a chorus in its prayer or ask help of responsive divinities "unless the Muse had produced a bard" (*vatem ni Musa dedis-set*).[11] The Greek Muse engenders a Roman bard, appropriate meshing of the double tradition from which the *Carmen* springs.

When considering the meaning of *carmen* in literary contexts it is well to note that the word is transgeneric. In its first appear-ance in Latin literature with the meaning "poetry," it refers to drama, in particular to tragedy,[12] and it is so used in the open-ing of the eighth *eclogue* of the stage productions of that poem's unnamed dedicatee.[13] Virgil's *Georgics* document appearances of *carmina* to define pastoral poetry (*carmina pastorum*) as well as didactic (*Ascraeum carmen*).[14] As for elegy, Tibullus made use of *carmina* in 2. 5. 2 in connection with Apollo's inspirational epiphany, but the poet is even more explicit about the power of song (or in this case its impotence) at 2. 4. 13 where he bemoans the lack of efficacy his verse betrays in his affair with Nemesis:

> nec prosunt elegi nec carminis auctor Apollo . . .

> neither are my elegies of any help nor Apollo creator
> of my song.

We find the same heady mixture of *carmen* as both magic song and formal elegiac verse, with each often shading into the other, throughout the Propertian corpus.[15]

For *carmina* and epic, Virgil offers a series of instances. Let me single out two. At *Aen.* 7. 734, the speaker addresses Oebalus, introducing him with the line

> Nec tu carminibus nostris indictus abibis,
> Oebale, . . .

> Nor will you withdraw unmentioned from our verses, Oebalus[16]

Apostrophe, especially in epic where third-person narrative is the rule, has the effect of bringing its object immediately before us, of abstracting it from the impersonality of ongoing storytelling and giving it special vividness. Direct address in such a setting brings specificity and with it a form of immortality. This immortality is complemented and reinforced by Virgil's mention of *carminibus nostris*. He means, of course, the fact that Oebalus figures in the *Aeneid,* and the sempiternity of the whole guarantees the endurance of its parts. Because the poem is a masterpiece of the literary imagination, it ensures that its creations forever flourish. Yet *carmina* signify not only the "songs" that Virgil sings—*arma virumque cano*—but the power behind them, the magic energy that allows words to accomplish deeds. Virgil is perhaps most explicit about this potency of words at the extraordinary moment in *Aeneid* 9 that brings the Nisus and Euryalus episode to a conclusion. Both heroes have lost their lives as they attempted to cross the enemy lines in the quest for Aeneas. But bodily death is no match for the poet's eternal prestige:[17]

> Fortunati ambo! si quid mea carmina possunt,
> nulla dies umquam memori vos eximet aevo,

dum domus Aeneae Capitoli immobile saxum
accolet imperiumque pater Romanus habebit.

Blessed by fortune, both! If my songs have any
power, no day will ever take you away from time's
memory, while the house of Aeneas will cherish the
steady rock of the Capitolium and father Romanus
will hold commanding sway.

Once more we have apostrophe as the rhetorical figure commanding the continued presence of those addressed. Once again we have the claim that Virgil's *carmina* have the ability to immortalize. Here, in addition, the immortalizing power of poetry is supplemented by its capacity to serve as a reminder, a *monimentum* for time to come, a time that in this context is closely associated with the permanence of Rome and its setting. But this literal and figurative ambiance draws not only on the explicit meaning of *carmina* as epic verses but also on their connotation as ritual charms that bring about permanence through the incantatory spell of words.

Finally, the significance of the word *carmen* in relation to the *Carmen Saeculare* takes a specifically Horatian turn, meaning for him lyric verse and in particular the first three books of odes, or, as the manuscripts entitle them, *Carmina*. *Epistle* 2. 2, addressed to Julius Florus and dated most probably to 19–18 B.C.E.—between the initial collections of odes (23 B.C.E.) and epistles (20 B.C.E.) and the *Carmen*—provides more specifics. In the epistle Horace three times refers to the writing of *carmina* and on each occasion, whether implicitly or explicitly, compares them to another genre. In the first instance (25) he suggests a contrast of the *carmina,* that is, lyric poetry, that Florus (no doubt having *Odes* I–III in mind) had expected from the poet, with the elaborate epistle that came his way instead.

At lines 59–60 Horace turns directly to Florus:

carmine tu gaudes, hic delectatur iambis,
ille Bioneis sermonibus et sale nigro.

You take pleasure in (lyric) song, this person finds
delight in iambic verse, that one in satires like Bion's
and in black salt.

Florus' own prejudice is toward lyric poetry, which, the inti-
mation is, he may also have written. The predilection of others
leans either toward invective or satiric verse, that is, toward what
Horace had already accomplished in his earlier *Epodes* and two
books of *Satires*.[18] Finally we turn to the speaker himself and to
the much-discussed passage later in the poem where he compares himself to Alcaeus and a fellow poet, nameless but most
likely Propertius, to Callimachus (91): *carmina compono, hic ele-
gos* ("I compose lyric poetry, this [other poet] elegies"). In all
three instances Horace is using the word *carmen* to define lyric
verse, by careful contradistinction to epistles, to poetry written
in iambs, to satiric verse and elegy, and in the first and last examples, he is asking the word *carmina* to allude specifically to his
own lyric masterpiece, the extraordinary collection of odes that
he had gathered for publication some five years previously.[19]

This threefold heritage of the word *carmen* influences the title
of the *Carmen Saeculare* and therefore the import of the poem
itself. It looks in particular to what Horace had already achieved
in the genre of lyric and therefore brings to bear both the force
and significance of *Odes* I–III as he returns to lyric with an
ode that in a variety of ways stands unique. Seen in more general terms, the word carries with it all past poetry, irrespective
of genre, and therefore the dynamism of the poetic imagination, from Homer to Horace himself. Finally *carmen* exerts on
Horace's singular enterprise its most basic meaning, a meaning
that transcends the specificity of poetry, of something sung in
order to charm, whether the intent be positive or negative. In

this instance we bear witness to a song that by the incantatory spell of words duly delivered in proper ritual form can "induce" the presence of the gods and physically engender that for which it prays.

The *Carmen,* as we have seen, is part of a continuous tradition of hymnic performance that, in the case of the songs of the Salic priests and of the Arval brethren, goes back to Rome's earliest recorded history. It is also a salient example of another tradition involving the singing of hymns, namely, the commissioning of songs to the gods when heaven's intervention to help Rome was considered crucial. The *Ludi Tarentini,* ancestors of Augustus' *Ludi Saeculares,* form part of this picture. One of Horace's most creative alterations to this complex inheritance is a question of tonality. Where the majority of such performances in the past came about because negative circumstances needed amelioration, Horace, by contrast, can celebrate the status quo and immortalize it through his song. His magic, once more, will prove to be sympathetic — not apotropaic — granting reassurance of the quality of the present rather than praying away evil in the hope of a better future.

Let us begin with the year 348 B.C.E., which, if the hypothesis of Lily Ross Taylor is correct, marked the initial occurrence of the *Ludi Tarentini.*[20] Taylor bases her argument on Livy's mention of a pestilence that year, causing the *Decemviri sacris faciundis* to consult the Sibylline books and hold a *lectisternium* of supplication to the gods. Many of the elements that would call for, or initiate, the *Ludi* are in place, not least their origin in the need to make expiation to the gods for whatever has caused the outbreak of disease. We are on firmer ground with the *Ludi* of 249. Pseudo-Acro, drawing on the work of the erudite Augustan scholar Verrius Flaccus,[21] states that in that year *ludi* were celebrated to Dis and Proserpina because part of the city wall had been struck by lightning and so that the war with

Carthage might proceed successfully. (The implication is that matters were not faring well, and in fact during the year 249 the Romans suffered severe losses in sea battles off Sicily.) The Sibylline books were again consulted by the *Decemviri*, a *sacrificium* was offered, and a *carmen saeculare* performed. Once again we have *Ludi* presented during a time of trial in order to avert the negative implications of a *prodigium* and to alter the ill fortunes of war. For the first time we have a *carmen* associated with the *Ludi* and, given the context, we presume it had an apotropaic quality.[22]

The documentation for the one set of *Ludi* that occurred between 249 and Augustus' games in 17 adds little to our knowledge of the *Ludi*. The chief bone of scholarly contention about them is whether they are to be dated to 149 or to 146. The evidence of Livy, and the fact that the games would have been repeated after exactly a hundred years, favor the former date. The discussion in Censorinus, where he quotes the historian Cassius Hemina who would have been writing contemporaneously with the event, is evidence for the latter chronology.[23] If the date 149 is correct, the Romans might well have been calling on the gods to better their fortunes in the attempt to eradicate Carthage, for the events in the first two years of the Third Punic War were not encouraging. If we accept the date 146, then the games would have been in thanksgiving for the war's positive outcome and would therefore offer the only evidence before Augustus' *Ludi* that such games were celebratory.

Until 17 B.C.E. a *carmen* is mentioned only in connection with the games of 249. There is growing evidence, however, that during the late Republic individual hymns were performed in times of difficulty. The most famous comes in Livy's report for the year 207. An extraordinary number of ugly portents and prodigies (among others, the city's wall was again struck by lightning) prompted the senate to decree that a song should be chanted through the city by a chorus of twenty-seven virgins. The author was none other than Livius Andronicus, the "founder" of Roman letters ("the song was composed by the poet Livius," *conditum ab Livio poeta carmen*).[24] Seven years later, under similar circumstances, the Sibylline books were consulted and another series of propitiatory rites ordered. This time the hymn was composed by P. Licinius Tegula.[25] As for the subsequent history of such songs, we learn from Julius Obsequens, no doubt culling from books of Livy now lost, of two other later occasions where a chorus of virgins offered a song in response to a troubling prodigy. The first was in 119 ("three-times-nine virgins chanted in the city," *virgines ter novenae in urbe cantarunt*), and the second in 117, in similar circumstances ("twenty-seven virgins purified the city with their song," *virgines viginti septem urbem carmine lustraverunt*).[26]

If the *Ludi* of 149–46 were celebrated in the latter year as an act of public rejoicing, they form the only exception to a general picture that we can draw in Republican history from a survey of the performances of *Ludi*, of a *carmen* chanted in connection with them, and of *carmina* sung on other public occasions. All such performances are associated with what we might call ill-omened or maleficent events. The *Ludi* apparently have their origin at a time of pestilence, and their recurrence, as is the case with all the other presentations of parallel *carmina*, happens when prodigies or disease or a negative turn in political circumstances demand that the gods be appeased.

Both the literary and historical evidence therefore converge to form a composite picture of the background against which Horace wrote his *Carmen*. Indeed, not too long before he received the commission for the *Carmen* Horace wrote *c*. 1. 21 about the production of a hymn to Apollo and Diana that ends by asking the god to send tearful war, miserable starvation, and disease away from people and prince to Rome's enemies. We are still in a spiritual world where a hymn can serve an apotropaic function as well as that of paean or eulogy. And three years at the most before the *Carmen*'s performance Tibullus wrote his most "Roman" elegy, addressed to Apollo Palatinus, in which the god, now mild of heart, must be supplicated to submerge recent prodigies, of which the poet has just given us an impressive list, "underneath untamed waters:"

> . . . sed tu iam mitis, Apollo,
> prodigia indomitis merge sub aequoribus.[27]

In terms of both the historical background of the presentation of *carmina* and of Horace's literary heritage, the *Carmen Saeculare* breaks from traditional tonality in order strictly to emphasize the positive elements in Rome's new secular dispensation under Augustus. There is no cause, now, for the gods to be conciliated and every reason why they should be asked to assure the continuity of a glorious present. The *Carmen* works its lexical and rhetorical magic to accomplish this goal during the course of the poem. Finally, the changes that Horace brings to this multivalent heritage sustain and confirm the notable alterations that Augustus makes to the larger heritage of performance of the *Ludi*, which are no longer *Tarentini* but *Saeculares*. Although some of the ceremonies did take place at the Tarentum on the western edge of the Campus Martius, a major portion of them was transferred to the Palatine and Capitoline. Likewise the divinities of consequence were changed from Dis and Proserpina to Apollo and Diana. We move from river valley to hill's crest, from worship of divinities of underworld and death to celestial beings who inform not only light- and life-giving sun and moon but also grant health and fertility to earth and its creatures and inspire poets to their highest levels of accomplishment. Again, negative becomes positive and, through a poet's power, we avert our glance from any troubling visions to embrace the Augustan world, its gods, and its dreams.

The *Carmen Saeculare* is an easy poem to damn with faint praise. On the most literal level it can be taken as purely evidentiary, that is, as an important piece of documentation for one of the major events of the Augustan principate, the presentation of the *Ludi Saeculares* in 17 B.C.E. The *Carmen,* as it were, expands on the phrase *Carmen composuit Q. Horatius Flaccus* in the *Acta,* fleshing out a significant detail in the epigraphical description of the event. It is likewise facile to politicize the poem, to see it, yet again, as evidence, in this case for Augustan moral reform as well as for the imprinting of Augustan ideology on Roman intellectual history, in the prominence given Apollo, say, or, on the human level, in the intimacy that lyric extends between Aeneas and Augustus.

But Horace is creating a world for politics, not serving as a henchman to the mighty or as an aesthetic toady. He is exerting a poet's power not only to imagine what the Roman polis should be but to bring that vision into being by means of his originality, whether in the poem's grand sweep or in the emphases of bright detail.

A listing of some topics that we might expect to find in such a poem but do not reveals Horace's inventiveness. Mention of *fraus* brings with it a depiction of Aeneas' scathelessness, not of Laomedon's deceit of the gods (one of Rome's two ancestral wrongs). Romulus is alluded to not as initiator of civil war (Rome's other inherited moral offense) or as offerer of violence to the Sabine women in order to expand his population but merely as the giver of his name to the race of Romans. The seven heights of the city are hills, not walls or citadels, with the implications of militarism such designations bring, and Apollo appears with arrow safely in its quiver and therefore not as god of disease or hunt or martial prowess with a propensity for vendetta, but as protector of Rome, its progeny, and its poet. We are in a post-Actium, post-*Aeneid* world where the journey to either the old or the renewed Rome is over, where the negative resentments of the gods are past and where Anchises' imperative to his son, as surrogate for all Roman users of political strength, to establish a custom for peace, has now become a reality. There are now no prodigies anticipating dire events to be exorcised by apotropaic song or diseases to be warded off, only a world of positive values confirmed by the poet's verse.

How does this magic work? How does the poet's opus, that manufactures the *opus* of Rome, gain its distinctive vigor? Part of its spiritual energy derives from what I have called the cooptation of other languages. We have the language of the Sibyl, first in the hexameters preserved by Phlegon and Zosimus prescribing the *Ludi*, and then as inherited from the poetry of Virgil and Tibullus. From Virgil's fourth *eclogue* Horace gleans, expands, and brings to fruition the notion of the age of Cumaean song, which means a renewal of the *saeclorum ordo,* and it is of course the agency of the Sibyl, in *Aeneid* 6, that allows Aeneas to learn of future Rome and Augustus, again anticipating what Horace brings to reality. The Sibyl likewise speaks in Tibullus 2. 5 in the language of prophecy that Horace again absorbs and, secondhand, in the language of prodigy that Horace shuns.

There is also the language of the Fates, given voice at lines 25–29 and in rich response to Catullus and Virgil. From Catullus' sixty-fourth poem Horace assimilates the epithalamium sung by the Fates but reverses its tonality. Instead of a misfortunate wedding boycotted by Apollo and Diana that produced a hero who in Latin letters regularly incorporates war's barbarism and anticipated an era of severe moral decline for mortals, we have a ceremony in which Apollo and Diana can rejoice, sporting a symbolic union in which they can share and a series of birthings they can secure, be they of children generally or of the particular lineage of Aeneas and Rome. In *eclogue* 4 Horace witnesses the future career of a *puer* who, after enduring the reappearance of the *Argo* and of Achilles, can bring about an era of nobility for humankind. As the poem nears its end, Virgil's Parcae, in language varied from Catullus, announce the imminence of an optimistic age. Horace conjures it into being.

This double heritage forms part of what we might call more generally the language of ceremony. In terms of genre Horace's poem involves the legacy of hymn inherited from both the Greek and Roman past. More specifically, the *Carmen Saeculare* looks not only to past performances of the *Ludi* but to the history of singing *carmina* documented for us from the Twelve Tables on. Our investigation of the word *carmen* in turn shows how its adoption draws with it most previous formal Latin poetry where the creative potential of song is ever imminent, in particular Horace's own *Carmina*.

A study of Horace's language in the *Carmen* reveals special moments of originality. Sometimes words are totally new (*Genitalis*) or newly metaphoric (*munivit iter*). Sometimes diction is novel so that the Latin lexicon is refreshed. We have the first use of the adjective *almus* with a male divinity, of *maritus* as an adjective meaning "related to marriage," and of *verax* with the infinitive. *Albanus* for the first time signifies Roman and not just belonging to Alba Longa as a historical station on the way to Rome: by the poet's metonymical origination Alba is co-opted into Rome. We observe in several instances the evolution of language, which is also to marvel at poetry's generative capability. Lines 17–20, for instance, illustrate the developmental linguistic interrelationship of *producas, prosperes, subolis,* and *prolis,* and the etymology of such words as *Parca, veneratur,* and *impetret* shares in inspiriting their contexts. The connection of the first with *pario* is doubly expressive: first, because it occurs in a context that is concerned with birth; second, because it lends emphasis to Horace's choice, in naming the Fates, of Parcae instead of Moerae, which is their designation in both the Sibylline verses and the *Acta* inscription. His word choice also cements the connection with Catullus 64 and the fourth *eclogue.*

In the *Carmen* Horace displays his fondness of anagrammatical play that here, as in the case of his employment of *figura etymologica,* also complements neatly the poem's stress on generative quality whereby language itself reinforces the growth of humankind and the expansiveness of Roman history. For Apollo *idem* and *diem* support each other as the god's clear sun symbolizes a new day that is both different from and equivalent to its predecessors. Likewise the parallel between *turmae* and *mutare,* in a context dealing with the migration of power from Troy to Rome, offers an example of how the iconicity of verbal change illuminates its context. Transformation in letters (or in the words they form) explicates the engendering, evolving metamorphoses of history, as Troy leads to Rome and Aeneas to Augustus. Once more, as in the case of *idem, diem,* and Apollo, language abets larger scaffoldings of meaning in which the community of sameness and change is critical.

All these instances of linguistic novelty, of etymological figuration or of anagrammatical play, remind us, synecdochically, that we are dealing with the parturition of Rome through the birth of words and that the potentiality of language, and of the ritual it both serves and creates, is fleshing out the germination and growth of Augustan Rome and the history that unfolds into it. The enacting dynamism of the word and the performative nature of poetry are never more clearly operative in ancient verse than in the *Carmen Saeculare.* And with the engendering aspects of language go Horace's modifications to the generic traditions of hymn, especially at the poem's ending where we attend to the elimination of apostrophe and to the change from subjunctives and imperatives to indicatives as the poet's sorcery takes hold.

Meter, here, is a form of metaphor. We expect a rhythm of Pindaric complexity or at the least Alcaics to fit the grand solemnity of the *Carmen*, a public song at the point of climax of a public celebration of Rome's historical renewal. Why, then, does Horace turn to Sapphics, which we expect as complement to a lyric of personal nature, dealing with private response to private emotion? My suggestions for the reasoning behind Horace's choice are two. We are now in a post-Alcaic world, just we are in an era after the *Aeneid*, when tyranny's mutability and war's violence have yielded to a ceremonial for birth and regeneration. We must also remember that, unlike the lyric poetry of archaic Greece, the *Carmen* was written as well as spoken, to be taken in by the eye in solitary contemplation as well as by the ears of those lucky few who attended the unique duet of public performances on the Palatine and Capitoline. The ode's immediate survival depends on writing that grants it the same lien on permanence as the *Carmen* gives to Rome, eternal even now in the minds of Horace's readers.

Horace's usage of myth also attains the status of metaphor by playing with the reader's expectation. For instance, when Aeneas first enters the poem he is associated with *libertas*, as "builder of a road for freedom," and is styled *castus*, not *pius*, as Virgil would have led us to anticipate. Aeneas' *pietas* is implicit in the immediately subsequent description of Augustus who is given the label "offspring of Anchises and Venus" as he sacrifices the white bulls. It is the emperor, Aeneas' putative descendant, who puts his ancestral piety to work during the *Ludi*'s Palatine ritual.

Aeneas' unexpected *castitas* links him with the purity of the *Carmen*'s singers (*castos*, 6), and vice versa. The beginning of the poem's first half, concerned so deeply with Rome's present regeneration, finds counterbalance near the start of its second, which centers on the history that brought Rome from Troy to the present. In terms of temporality the balance is chiastic because it is Aeneas, the founding father, who in Horace's vision serves as exemplification of chastity for the young of modern Rome. Myth, therefore, in its generalizing capacity, functions as an aspect of Horace's educational task in the *Carmen*, with Aeneas proposed as model for *libertas* and *castitas* just as Augustus stands for *lenitas* in the exertion of dominion and, unexpectedly but by clear innuendo, for the *pietas* by which Virgil had marked Aeneas.

Finally we have poetic structure as metaphor. Like many great poems the *Carmen Saeculare* is built on a combination of circularity, where verbal echoes and stylistic repetitions confirm ring-composition, and linearity. For the first, both the conclusion of the poem's first half and its finale hark back with care to its opening stanzas. Linearity helps us perceive how the second half is built on the first, as we turn from the nameless births of the Augustan present to the history of Rome and the particularity of its progress from Aeneas to the emperor himself. Closure comes as the prayerful "we" of the chorus' opening lines becomes an amalgamated, assured "I" who carries home the certain hope that the song has satisfactorily dispatched its function.[28]

Rome, mimicking the disposition of the poem that tells of it, is built on sameness and change, on evolution and continuity, on rejuvenation and process as well as stability. Like the *saeculum* that the poem celebrates, Rome is maintained by births and rebirths, by repetitions of ceremony that initiate the new. The *Carmen* tells of Rome's persistence but also of its need for the regularity of ritual renovation. It also tells in summary much about the novelty of Augustus' *Ludi*, concerned not to pray away affliction or adversity but to rejoice in the present, to corroborate its moral quality with the help of epiphanic gods, and to teach this excellence through the mouthpiece of a supreme poet.

The *Carmen Saeculare* is one of the extraordinary poems about those eternal verities, place and time. As to place, we move from details of Apollo's temple on the Palatine, to the Sun's gaze on the majesty of the city and its hills, to Latium and the mountains that bound it, and thence to the further limits of the empire— all as correlatives of the ode's linearity.[29]

In looking at temporality, we range from the specific moment of celebration (and the duration of the poem's telling), exact but transient, to the eternity of the gods who bless the occasion. In between we have Rome for which we pray a share in that endurance but which is nevertheless fabricated from a series of individual births, be they those of the Roman present or of individuals from Aeneas to his glorious heir.

Time is also clocked by mention of *lustrum* and *melius aevum* at 67–68 into which Apollo will prolong, and advance, Roman civilization. The first can be both specific and general, a five-year period (associated with the taking of the census and accompanying rites of purification) or any grand extent of time. *Aevum* looks also to duration of time, specifically to that of a man's life. In such a sense it corresponds in meaning to *saeculum* and points to the iteration of the secular celebration itself, which contains within it both differentiations from past performances and yet necessary continuity as well. We thus, through Horace's genius, have the timely, and timeful, merged before us with the timeless as we scan the ongoing, developmental aspects of Roman might *sub specie aeternitatis,* that is, under the caring eye of divinities who will affirm the permanence of its fecundity. The *Carmen Saeculare*'s reconciliation of past, present, and future is the vatic poet's greatest exercise of his charm's potency, lifting the singularity of a unique public performance to the level of universal work of art.

Notes

In addition to the standard abbreviations for periodicals used by *L'Année philologique* (Paris, 1924–), the following appear in the notes:

FGH   *Die Fragmente der griechischen Historiker,* ed. F. Jacoby (Leiden, 1923–).
OCD   *Oxford Classical Dictionary* (Oxford: 2d ed., 1970; 3d ed., 1996).
OLD   *Oxford Latin Dictionary* (Oxford, 1968–82).
RE   *Real-Encyclopädie der classischen Altertumswissenschaft,* ed. A. Pauly, G. Wissowa, and W. Kroll (Stuttgart, 1893–).
RG   *Res Gestae Divi Augusti,* ed. P. Brunt and J. Moore (Oxford, 1967).
TLL   *Thesaurus Linguae Latinae* (Munich, 1900–).

CHAPTER 2
Horatian Background

1. These are also the odes in the collection that most suggest any irony on Horace's part directed toward the emperor and his family. See Putnam (1986), 244–45, on *c.* 4. 14.
2. *Aen.* 1. 294–96.
3. *C.* 4. 15. 17–19.
4. The ode's last word is *canemus,* "we will sing."
5. Here the "Roman" odes that open book 3 are only the apparent exceptions which prove the rule.
6. I follow for Horace the text established by F. Klingner (*Q. Horati Flacci: Opera,* 3d ed. [Leipzig, 1959]).
7. The main thrust of criticism on *c.* 1. 17 in recent decades is to view it as constructing an idealized spiritual landscape, where nature's freedom and abundance serves as metaphor for a world of art. See in particular: F. Klingner, "Horazerklärungen," *Philologus* 90 (1935): 289–93, repr. in *Römische Geisteswelt,* 5th ed. (Munich, 1965), 412–81; Fraenkel, 205–7; Commager, 348–52; I. Troxler-Keller, *Die Dichterlandschaft des Horaz* (Heidelberg, 1964), 108–18; A. W. J. Holleman, "Horace *Odes,* I, 17

and the 'Music of Love,'" *Latomus* 29 (1970): 750–55; H. G. Edinger, "Horace, *C*. 1. 17," *CJ* 66 (1970–71): 306–11; E. A. Schmidt, "Das horazische Sabinum als Dichterlandschaft," *A&A* 23 (1977): 97–112; D. Gagliardi, "*Pietas et musa* in Hor. *Carm.* 1, 17," *Vichiana* 11 (1982): 139–42; P. G. Toohey, "The Structure and Function of Horace, Odes 1.17," *ICS* 7 (1982): 110–24.

Horace's potential rejection of elegy is an important component in the analyses of H.-P. Syndikus, *Die Lyrik des Horaz,* vol. 1 (Darmstadt, 1972), 188–98, esp. 196–97, and Toohey, "Structure and Function," 113–15.

The erotic elements in the poem are a particular focus of the commentary of K. Quinn (*Horace: The Odes* [Basingstoke, 1980]) who sees it as the speaker's urbane and ironic invitation to Tyndaris to leave Rome and to spend the weekend with him in his Sabine retreat. R. Minadeo (*The Golden Plectrum: Sexual Symbolism in Horace's Odes* [Amsterdam, 1982]), 57–60, argues that the speaker wants to avert the problems of sexuality from his setting. Two recent readings take an opposite viewpoint. P. Pucci, ("Horace's Banquet in *Odes* 1. 17," *TAPA* 105 [1975]: 259–81) finds that the speaker "cannot avoid contemplating and describing [Cyrus'] assault" (275) in order to co-opt his rival's place in the affections of Tyndaris. F. M. Dunn, ("An Invitation to Tyndaris: Horace, *Ode* I.17," *TAPA* 120 [1990]: 203–8) adopts a still stronger stand, finding in the speaker someone "who pursues the woman he would protect and who turns from kind reassurance to verbal threats" (208), collapsing the difference between the speaker and his rival. Although my approach to the ode diverges in differing ways from each of these articles, I have learned much from both.

8. I do not share the view of Nisbet and Hubbard (216) that the representation of Tyndaris alters over the course of the poem from dream-figure to singer-courtesan.

9. For the etymology of Pan, see *RE* supp. 8. 951 (Brommer). Latin etymologies are collected by R. Maltby (*A Lexicon of Ancient Latin Etymologies,* Arca 25 [Leeds, 1991], 226). For Faunus, see A. Ernout and A. Meillet *Dictionnaire étymologique de la Langue Latine* (Paris, 1959), 221, as well as the citations collected by Maltby, which largely connect the name with *fari* (though cf. Serv. auc. on Virg. *geo.* 1. 10: *quidam faunos putant dictos ab eo, quod frugibus faveant*).

10. With the natural setting of *c*. 1. 17 we might compare the description of the Sabine farm in *epi.* 1. 16 where the (very Horatian) speaker tells of mountains that would be unbroken (*continui montes*) if they weren't separated by a shady valley (*opaca valle,* 5–6). He describes the whole as *hae latebrae dulces et . . . amoenae* (15).

11. On the word play see, e.g., Edinger, "Horace, *C.* 1. 17," 30 and, for its Var-ronian source, N. Horsfall, *Virgilio: l'epopea in alambicco* (Naples, 1991), 112.

   Virgil makes use of the same pun in *Aeneid* 8 during the description of Evander's walk with Aeneas through Pallanteum (343–44):

   > . . . et gelida monstrat sub rupe Lupercal,
   > Parrhasio dictum Panos de more Lycaei.

   > and he points out the Lupercal under the chill rock, named according to the Arcadian custom of Lycaean Pan.

12. I do not find convincing the conclusion Schmidt ("Das horazische Sa-binum als Dichterlandschaft," 101–2) draws by comparison to *c.* 3. 18. 13 (*inter audacis lupus errat agnos*) that Faunus is by definition a Wolfsab-wehrer. It is only on the festival of Pan-Faunus that such an *adunaton* occurs. Rather I would suggest that when Horace's Pan becomes Faunus by exchanging Arcadia for the Sabine territory, he forgoes his character as *Lykaios*. Roman "Pan" cannot be *lupercus* in Horace's sequestered vale. There is (doubly) no Mars in the context of *c.* 1. 17.

13. *C.* 1. 1. 21.

14. *C.* 1. 1. 30.

15. *Epi.* 1. 3. 21 .

16. *C.* 4. 2. 27–32. These last two passages are quoted by V. Buchheit, ("Ein-flüsse Vergils auf das Dichterbewusstsein des Horaz: III: Einladung beim Dichter (*c.* 1,17)," *SO* 63 [1988]: 77–94), 79, as part of a discussion of the poetic symbols in Horace's landscape.

17. *Ecl.* 7. 46 (and cf. *geo.* 2. 215–16 et, al.).

18. Nisbet and Hubbard offer no example of green snakes in Latin literature before Statius' *Thebaid*.

19. *Ecl.* 3. 93.

20. *C.* 3. 25. 3.

21. *DRN* 1. 926–27, cited also by Quinn (*Horace*), who also finds in *devio* a "symbol of poetry which is unprecedented."

22. 64. 332

23. *Aen.* 7. 349. *Levis* in this sense is always applied to a woman unless youth or effeminacy in a man is the subject (*OLD* s.v. 2 offers Ovid *A. A.* 3. 437 as an example of the latter usage).

24. *Aen.* 6. 703 (and cf. 679, *convalle virenti*) and 8. 609.

25. On *aestus* cf. *DRN* 5. 1435 and Préaux on Hor. *epi.* 1. 2. 8.

26. Nisbet and Hubbard, on line 22.

27. *C.* 1. 33. 6.

28. *C.* 3. 29. 27–28. Several other details link *c.* 1. 17 with *c.* 3. 29, among them the latter's mention of Procyon (18), a star in Canis Major, as herald of summer heat, parallel to that which Canicula (Sirius or its constellation, Canis Major) brings in *c.* 1. 17. 17–18.

29. Many of these parallels are mentioned by Troxler-Keller, *Die Dichterland-schaft*, 113, as part of a discussion of the poem's ring-composition.

30. There is no necessary "evolution" from *fistula* to *fides*. Both the pipe and the lyre appear twice elsewhere in Horace's poetry as joint accompaniments for *convivium* or celebration (*c.* 3. 19. 20; 4. 1. 22–24).

31. *C.* 4. 11. 31. The subtle kinship between the song-writing speaker and Phyllis who will sing these songs is established at the start of the poem when we learn that the speaker has at home "parsley for weaving crowns" (*nectendis apium coronis*, 3). Both protagonists will share crowns appropriate for the *convivium* and for the poets and poetry that will grace it.

 For more general discussions of parity as a major component of Epicurean definitions of friendship, see B. Frischer, *The Sculpted Word* (Berkeley, 1982), esp. 75–76, and P. Mitsis, *Epicurus' Ethical Theory: The Pleasure of Invulnerability* (*Cornell Studies in Classical Philology* 48: Ithaca, 1988). Toohey ("Structure and Function," 115) summarizes his convincing view that "Horace's Epicureanism precluded any real sympathy for the elegiac mode." On the intellectual level as well, Cyrus fails to complement the world that Horace conjures up for Tyndaris and his speaker.

32. *Epi.* 1. 5. 24–25.

33. Ibid., 25–26.

34. On the equivalence of wine and song in the poetry of Horace see the seminal article by S. Commager, "The Function of Wine in Horace's Odes," *TAPA* 88 (1957): 68–80, as well as Toohey, "Structure and Function," 117.

35. On Horace's uses of Anacreon see, e.g., the comments of Shorey on *c.* 1. 17. 18 and of Porphyrio on *c.* 1. 27. 1. Cf. also Anacreon fr. 57 (Campbell) dealing with the Bassarids of Dionysus with reference to *candide Bassareu* in line 11 of the subsequent ode.

36. On the iconography of Anacreon in archaic vase painting as typifying "a certain kind of Dionysiac minstrel," see Davis, 74 (on *epode* 14. 10) and the detailed discussion of F. Frontisi-Ducroux and F. Lissarrague, "De l'ambiguité à l'ambivalence," *Annali del seminario di studi del mondo classico* 5 (1983): 11–32.

37. On this point, see P. Rosenmeyer, *The Poetics of Imitation: Anacreon and*

the *Anacreontic Tradition* (Cambridge, 1992), esp. 106-14 on "The Code of Limitations" (106-9 deal specifically with myth).

38. *Sat.* 1. 10. 48-49.

39. Davis (204) comments as follows: "The disorderly behavior that erupts in the imaginary countersymposium is fraught with symbolic import. The violence to Tyndaris' wreath and raiment is an incisive warning of the consequences of transgressing the rule of *mediocritas*." I would add only that the production of poetry—and the protection of poets—is also a major concern of the speaker.

40. That the "clinging crown" simply evidences the fact that Tyndaris is not in love is the view of R. J. Seager ("Horace, Odes 1. 17. 24-8," *LCM* 3 [1978]: 201-2).

41. Cat. 51. 5.

42. Sappho 31. 5.

43. Sappho 31. 3-4.

44. For recent critiques of *c.* 3. 13, see esp. Commager, 323-24; Fitzgerald, 93-101; Davis, 126-32.

45. See, e.g., Williams (1969), 89.

46. *DRN* 4. 1034 (= 1047, a line usually considered spurious, with the change of initial *qui ciet* to *incitat*). Cf. Hor. *Sat.* 2. 7. 49 of the penis (*turgentis caudae*).

47. *DRN* 4. 1050-51. On the implicit sexuality of *cornibus* cf. Ovid *Am.* 1. 8. 48, and Petr. *Sat,* 134. 11.

48. Cat. 4. 12.

49. *C.* 3. 4. 5-7.

50. *C.* 3. 4. 9-20.

51. *C.* 3. 4. 22-24.

52. *C.* 3. 4. 41.

53. See Davis, 98-107, for a more detailed discussion of the warrant through which the speaker brings authority to his tutorial stance.

54. *C.* 3. 29. 11-12: . . . *beatae/fumum et opes strepitumque Romae.* The adjective *beatus* is used with some irony given its other essential meaning as "happy."

55. *C.* 3. 29. 16.

56. *C.* 3. 29. 26.

57. *C.* 1. 1. 2. The careful echo is noted by Santirocco (166).

58. *C.* 3. 30. 1.

59. On *c.* 3. 30, see Putnam (1973); Woodman.

60. For a detailed discussion of one example of Horace's interlinking of ritual and art see Putnam (2000).

61. Cf. *C.* 1. 37. 31 for the use of *deduci* to describe Augustus' triumph of 29 B.C.E.
62. *C.* 3. 24. 27.
63. *C.* 3. 24. 25–26.
64. *C.* 3. 25 stands out by comparison, say, to *c.* 1. 2. There, if a certain canonization of the emperor is implied in the poem's ending, it is not the work of the speaker. Rather, for all its hyperbole, the ending implies a lecture to its lofty addressee: seek triumphs over, and revenge against, the Parthians, not against our Roman selves. The implication is that Augustus is not yet truly ready for the poet's deification.
65. *C.* 3. 3. 9–12. The manuscripts are equally divided between the readings *bibet* and *bibit* at line 12. I opt for the future because of the parallel at *c.* 3. 5. 2 (*habebitur*) where the reading is unquestioned.
66. *C.* 3. 6. 45–48.
67. There is scarcely any poem in the Greco-Roman literary tradition about whose circumstances of composition we know more than the *Carmen Saeculare.* We have the evidence of Censorinus (*DN* 16. 17. 13) on the history and performance of the *Ludi* (originally entitled probably *Ludi Tarentini*), and Zosimus (*Histories* 2. 1–6) gives details of the actual rites. (At 2. 5 he offers a summary of the ceremonies and at 2. 6. 1–37 quotes the Sibylline oracle that enjoined the celebration of 17 B.C.E., which is also quoted by Phlegon [*Makrobioi.* 4 in Jacoby, ed., *FGH* 257:F37]). Augustus (*RG* 22) himself mentions that he put on the *Ludi* with Agrippa as his colleague (*collega M. Agrippa, ludos saeculares . . . feci*), and we have the notice in Dio Cassius (54. 18) that these were the fifth set of games to be performed. But in this case we are particularly fortunate to have, largely well preserved, the inscription detailing the full *Acta* of Augustus' *Ludi* (*CIL* 6. 32323). At lines 147–48 we learn that a hymn (*carmen*) was sung by boys and girls on June 3, when the final offerings had been completed, first on the Palatine and then on the Capitolium. At line 149 we read: *Carmen composuit Q. Horatius Flaccus.*

    For a full discussion of the inscription, its discovery, initial publication, and interpretation, as well as of the poem's general historical background, see Fraenkel, 364–71. The "nuanced relationship" of the poem to the religious proceedings is sympathetically treated by Feeney (1998), 37.
68. Dio Cassius 54. 18. The historian also mentions that during the year 17 Augustus transferred the dates of the festival of Honor and Virtus, abstractions that appear prominently at *C. S.* 57–58, to those they presently occupy. The double temple to Honor and Virtus at the Porta Capena was of special importance to Augustus. It was *ante aedes Honoris et Virtutis*

that, he tells us (*RG* 11), the senate consecrated an altar to *Fortuna Redux* upon his return from Syria in October 19.

CHAPTER 3
The *Carmen Saeculare*

1. The extensive scholarship on the *Carmen* is surveyed in the bibliography. I have found the following particularly informative and stimulating: Arnold; Feeney (1998), 28–38; Fraenkel, 364–82; Galinsky (1996), 102–4; White, 123–27; Williams (1968), 57–61; Zanker, 171–97, in Shapiro, trans., 167–92.

2. For the phrase *lucidum caeli decus* in conjunction with *silvarumque potens,* cf. (as Kiessling and Heinze) *Aen.* 9. 405 where Nisus addresses Diana as *astrorum decus et nemorum Latonia custos.* In this case epic's private, nocturnal prayer is transferred to lyric's public acclaim.

3. Cf. Zosimus 2. 6. 6 ("when night has come to earth"). Horace gently countermands even the Sibyl's counsel just as he suppresses mention of the initial part of the celebration, which took place "at night in the meadow by the Tiber" (*nocte . . . in campo ad Tiberim*) where Augustus sacrificed nine ewes and nine she-goats to the Moerae at the Tarentum at the western end of the Campus Martius near the edge of the river where the inscription dealing with the *Acta* (see note 67 to chapter 2) was discovered in 1891 during the building of the permanent embankments.

4. Cf. also the *Acta* for June 2, stating that Augustus, "at night by the Tiber" (*noctu . . . ad Tiberim*), sacrificed a pregnant sow to *Terra Mater* and prayed for the Roman citizenry (*CIL* 6. 32323. 134–37). The only animal sacrifice mentioned in the *Carmen* is of *bobus albis* (49) presumably to the *di* of 45–46, who may include Jupiter and Juno as well as Apollo and Diana.

5. Fraenkel (378) forgets the initial *precamur* when he states that only at the end of the poem does the chorus speak "in its own name." The "we" of the opening stanza is carefully delineated.

6. Varro, *LL* 5. 7. 41 (*Ubi nunc est Roma, Septimontium nominatum ab tot montibus, quos postea urbs muris comprehendit*).

7. *Geo.* 2. 535, repeated at *Aen.* 6. 783 with the change from *circumdedit* to *circumdabit.* (Anchises is anticipating a future that has already occurred for the speaker of the *Georgics.*)

8. Tib. 2. 5. 55; Prop. 3. 11. 57. At 4. 1. 2, Propertius describes "mightiest Rome" (*maxima Roma*) as a combination of hill and grass (*collis et herba*). The Palatine, which may be included in the word *collis,* is described at 3–

4. It is sacred for its temple to *Navali Phoebo,* which is to say to Apollo as fosterer of the victory in the sea battle at Actium.

9. *F.* 1. 515. Cf. also *Tr.* 1. 5. 69–70 (*septem montibus*).

10. On the *moenia* motif in Latin literature, see M. Von Albrecht, *Silius Italicus: Freiheit und Gebundenheit römischer Epik* (Amsterdam, 1964), 24–26.

11. Mention of *colles* here and of *Palatinas aras* at 65 also highlights the absence of the Capitolium from the poem, though one of the performances of the *Carmen* took place there (*CIL* 6. 32323. 148; cf. also 103 and 119) and though the site of the temple of Jupiter Optimus Maximus stands regularly elsewhere in Horace as a symbol of Rome (e.g., *c.* 1. 37. 6, 3. 3. 42, 3. 24. 45, 3. 30. 8, 4. 3. 9). The *Carmen* belongs most immediately to the Palatine and its Apollo is Palatinus (cf. also *epi.* 1. 3. 17).

12. Cf. Vir. *Aen.* 6. 71 (with Austin's comment), dated with some assurance around 23 B.C.E., and Tib. 2. 5. 17–18, with the introductory note of K. F. Smith (ed., *The Elegies of Albius Tibullus* [New York, 1913]). The epigram of Domitius Marsus attached to the *Vita Tibulli* treats the death of the elegist as contemporary with that of Virgil, which took place in 19 B.C.E. Moreover, the position of Messalinus, as the last named of the *Quindecimviri* listed as celebrating the *Ludi* in the *Acta* (*CIL* 6. 32323. 152), suggests that his inauguration as *quindecimvir,* which Tib. 2. 5 memorializes, was recent.

According to Suetonius (*Aug.* 31. 1), Augustus deposited the Libri "in two gilded cases under the pedestal of the Palatine Apollo" (*duobus forulis auratis sub Palatini Apollonis basi*), which is to say under the interior statue of Apollo by Scopas (Pliny *HN* 36. 25), which was flanked by statues of Diana and Latona. Parke, 150, plausibly fixes the transference of the books to the date of the temple's dedication, Oct. 9, 28 B.C.E. The fact that a crouching figure of the Sibyl was almost certainly in front of Apollo further confirms the presence of the Libri. (For details, see P. Gros, "Apollo Palatinus," in *Lexicon Topographicum Urbis Romae,* ed. E. M. Steinby [Rome, 1993], 54–55.)

13. Horace may be thinking of the moment in *Aen.* 6 (872) when Anchises styles Rome a *magnam urbem* to his son. Seeing is important in both contexts, but Anchises is anticipating a future occasion when the city mourns the demise of Marcellus, Augustus' youthful heir and son-in-law. Death has no place in Horace's content.

14. Most recently Hardie (1993), 125–26, and Feeney (1998), 33.

15. Prop. 2. 31. 11. The "dramatic" date of the elegy is the moment of the opening of the Danaid portico adjacent to the Apollo temple. Since the

book was published no later than 26 B.C.E., the poem was presumably
written, and the portico dedicated, not long after the dedication of the
temple itself, which took place on October 9, 28 B.C.E.

16. Prop. 2. 31. 12–14.

17. See Ovid *A. A.* 1. 73–74:

> . . . quaque parare necem miseris patruelibus ausae
>> Belides et stricto stat ferus ense pater; . . .

> and where the descendants of Belus [i.e., the Danaids] dare to
> prepare death for their wretched cousins and where the ferocious
> father stands with drawn sword.

Ovid repeats line 74 at *Tr.* 3. 1. 62 with the change of *stat ferus* to *barbarus*,
as if further to underscore the ruthless madness of Danaus' posture. Line
73 strongly suggests that his daughters were to be seen acting in response
to or, better, echoing their father's mood.

The form and placement of the portico has been most recently ex-
amined by L. Balensiefen ("Überlegungen zu Aufbau und Lage der
Danaidenhalle auf dem Palatin," *MDAIR* 102 [1995]: 189–209). The
evidence of Ovid, however, would seem to argue against her essentially
pacific view of the monument.

18. *Almam meam nutricem* (Pl. *Curc.* 358)

19. See R. D. Williams, ed., *P. Vergili Maronis Aeneidos: Liber Quintus*
(Oxford, 1960) on *Aen.* 5. 64f.

20. The importance of the theme of birth is also noted by Arnold, esp.
482–86.

21. Michael Paschalis reminds me that, generally speaking, the sun's glorious
gleam forms both a contrast to the poet's treatment of the heavenly body
in *c.* 1–3 and an anticipation of its appearances in *c.* 4 where its public
role is paramount. In *c.* 1–3 Horace regularly suggests our need to escape
from the sun and the menaces its heat symbolizes. In *c.* 4, by contrast, the
sun lends authority to the day of Caesar's return (*c.* 4. 2) and outlines a
day of praise in his honor (*c.* 4. 5); it reveals the civilized world (*c.* 4. 14)
and defines the extent of empire (*c.* 4. 15). The *Carmen Saeculare* effects
the transition from private apprehension of the sun's hurtful potential
to acknowledgment of its value as bright, public emblem of Augustus,
the worshipful Increaser, and of the day on which he chose to reinforce
his nourishing role. The sun's omniscient power of observation reflects
not only the extent of Rome's domain but the poet's ability to waft us
into space and view what the sun views. It is an easy step to interconnect

this imaginative talent both with Apollo and with the grandly communal gesture which the writing and performance of the hymn represent.

22. Ovid *Am.* 2. 13. 21 is the only possible exception. The epithet is closely associated with Artemis in Greek cultic practice (see, e.g., W. Burkert, *Greek Religion* [Cambridge, 1985], 170–73; *Der Neue Pauly* 3. 914–15 s.v. "Eilithyia" [Graf]). Dionysius of Halicarnassus (*Ant. Rom.* 4. 15.5) states that the Romans entitled Hera Eilithyia, i.e., Juno Lucina.

   For further details on the Latin merger of Eilithyia-Artemis and Diana, see F. Bömer, ed., *P. Ovidius Naso: Metamorphosen, Buch IV–V* (Heidelberg, 1976), on 5. 304; *Buch VIII–IX* (Heidelberg, 1977), 361 (on 9. 273–323).

23. The "u" sound alone we hear in *Ilithyia* and *lucina* whereas *rite*, with its reference to proper procedure, anticipates the subsequent *tu*.

24. The stanza is the most denigrated in the poem. "Pure prose," pronounces Shorey, one of Horace's most sympathetic commentators. The judgment of Williams (1968), 59, could serve as summary of negative views: "What is wrong [with the stanza] to modern taste is that the language is descriptive, analytical, matter-of-fact; the poet seems to have no vision to communicate, no emotion to share."

25. We are surely meant to hear an echo of Augustus' *Lex Iulia de maritandis ordinibus* in the phrase *lege marita*. (On the law, see Suet. *Aug.* 34; L. Raditsa, "Augustus' Legislation Concerning Marriage, Procreation, Love Affairs and Adultery," *ANRW* 2.13. (1980): 278–339, esp. 319–29; S. Treggiari, *Roman Marriage* [Oxford, 1991], 60–80.)

26. For *suboles* and *proles* as both archaic and solemn, and for the solemnity of *prosperare* as well, see Fraenkel, 375, n. 1.

27. Censorinus (*DN* 17. 2) defines a *saeculum* as "the longest extent of human life bounded by birth and death" (*spatium vitae humanae longissimum partu et morte definitum*). Cf. also the Sibylline oracle's announcement of the need to celebrate a new *saeculum* "when the longest span of life for men has passed, journeying through a hundred-and-ten year cycle" (Zosimus 2. 6. 1–2). The translation is by J. Ferguson in *Rome: The Augustan Age*, ed. K. Chisholm and J. Ferguson (Oxford, 1981), 150.

28. We notice how assonance and alliteration combine to reinforce the connection between "you" (*vos*), the Parcae and the veracity of their song, as *vos* leads to *ver-* and the "c" sounds interknit *veraces, cecinisse,* and *Parcae* (the last five letters of which are an anagram of the central letters of *veraces* just as the first five are included in *peractis* two lines later).

29. We should note also how the adjectival suffix they share unites *feraci* (19)

with *veraces* and adds to the aura of potentiality that permeates the two stanzas.

30. *"Nam 'Parca'* . . . *inmutata una littera, a partu nominata"* (*NA* 3. 16. 10).
31. *RR* 1. 1. 5.
32. The quatrains' rhetoric is also fused by the figural interassociations of *fertilis, frugum,* and *fetus.* Ovid (*F.* 4. 631-32) brings the etymological connection to the surface:

> forda ferens bos est fecundaque dicta ferendo;
> hinc etiam fetus nomen habere putant.
>
> *Forda* is a cow with calf (*ferens*) and is called fruitful (*fecunda*) from bearing (*ferendo*). Hence they also think that offspring (*fetus*) get their name.

At 4. 671-72 he links *fructum* with *fecundior* and *ferunt.*
33. E.g., Kiessling and Heinze on line 29.
34. Horace's may be the first use of *condo* in the sense of return an arrow to its quiver. *TLL* compares Ovid *R. A.* 612 and *F.* 2. 326 (*conditaque in pharetra tela*). Horace uses *telum* of an arrow at *c.* 4. 9. 17.
35. See esp. Hom. *Il.* 1. 43-47 where we are told that "arrows rattled on the shoulders of the god in his anger" (46).
36. *Tela sonant umeris* (*Aen.* 4. 149).
37. *Aen.* 8. 704. In line 33 Horace may be thinking of a moment earlier in book 8 (88) where the Tiber's waters, as Aeneas makes his way to Pallanteum, are compared to a "gentle" (*mitis*) pool or a "calm" (*placidae*) lake. This is the only occasion in Virgil where *mitis* and *placidus* are juxtaposed, as it is here in Horace. Each moment is concerned, in ways both general and particular, with the (re)birth of Rome after violence has passed.
38. Prop. 4. 1. 3 and 6. 67; Ovid *M.* 13. 715.
39. There is no mention, for instance, of Diana's share in the vengeance the twin divinities wreaked against Niobe. It is appropriate that Diana appear as the new moon in this poem so concerned with birth and fresh beginnings (cf. *nascente luna, c.* 3. 23. 2).
40. The word *opus* in this, the central stanza of the poem, has layers of significance. The immediate "work" is the crafting of Rome by the gods, the immortal undertaking that is implemented by Aeneas. But the *opus* is secondarily also the work of the poet whose artistry here can lyricize the *Aeneid* and, more generally, stabilize history's processes in the glorious "now" of the hymnic moment.

41. For *turmae* as squadrons of cavalry, see also *c*. 2. 16. 22 and cf. *c. 3*. 4. 47 (*mortalis turmas*).

One of the more provocative anagrams in the poem is the permutation of *turmae* (38) into *mutare* (39). The relocation from Ilium to the Etruscan shore is poetically reified in the change that the "throngs" themselves must experience. Likewise *cursu* (40) is contained within the center of *Etruscum* (38), helping further sonically knit together an extraordinarily blended stanza.

The original meaning of *turma*, according to Varro (*LL* 5. 91), is a squadron of thirty horsemen (*turma* from *terima* composed of *ter deni equites* from three tribes). The military aspect of *turma* is picked up later, e.g., in *manus* (53).

42. The richly metaphoric phrase *liberum munivit iter* (43) may have its source in Lucretius' *via . . . munita fidei* (*DRN* 5. 102), the "paved path of belief" that leads into the mind through the senses of sight and touch. Cf. also 3. 498, *munita viai*, the "paved way" of the particles of voice. Aeneas' voyage is at once both literal and spiritual, a moment in history's progress but also a symbol of the transfer of power and morality. The first literal use of the idiom *munire iter* seems to be by Nepos (*Han*. 3. 4).

43. The change from Troy to Italy, within a context dealing with Apollo and with the writing of the *Carmen*, is central also to *c*. 4. 6, an ode whose importance for understanding the *Carmen* we will examine shortly.

44. The rare, archaic adjective *sospes* makes suitable appearance in this context. According to A. Ernout and A. Meillet (*Dictionnaire étymologique de la Langue Latine* [Paris, 1959]) it is often joined to *salvus* and *superstes*, a connection confirmed by the use of *superstes* two lines later (42), uniting Aeneas' scatheless journey with his own holy survival.

45. See Cic. *Div*. 2. 98; Var. *RR* 2. 1. 9.

46. Tib. 2. 5. 89–90. See Prop. 4. 1. 14, 4. 4. 77–78 and Ovid *F*. 4. 781–82 as well as Smith, ed., *Elegies* 87–90, for further references to the custom of jumping through flames.

47. Ovid *F*. 4. 799–800

48. With *ardentem Troiam* cf. *Aen*. 7. 244 where Ilioneus speaks of Aeneas' offerings to Latinus as *reliquias Troia ex ardente receptas*. Aeneas as much as the objects he brings is part of these *reliquiae*.

49. Mention of Aeneas's *castitas* serves to underscore the nonerotic tone of the poem as a whole. When dealing with procreation, it is on paternity and maternity that the poet puts his emphasis. Reference to the conjunction of Anchises and Venus dwells not on their intimacy but on their progeny. Horace thereby raises an unspoken paradox deserving of fur-

ther scrutiny, namely, that in Virgil, Aeneas' *pietas* brings with it erotic connotations to be excluded from the present poem.

50. *Laomedonteae . . . periuria Troiae* (*geo.* 1. 502). Cf. *Aen.* 4. 542 (with the further citations of A. S. Pease, ed., *Publi Vergili Maronis Aeneidos: Liber Quartus* [Cambridge, 1935]) and 5. 811. The *fraus* at *ecl.* 4. 31 may well also be connected with Laomedon's treachery.

51. It is not completely implausible that Horace is raising the specter of the legend of Aeneas' treachery at Troy only to dismiss it as Virgil had. For the evidence, see Dio. Hal. *Ant. Rom.* 1. 48 (quoting Menecrates of Xanthus).

52. The ordered repetition of *di* (45–46) contrasts with the chiasmus that dominates the remainder of the lines: *probos mores docili iuventae* balancing *senectuti placidae quietem.* The contrast between *iuventae* and *senectuti* is furthered in those between *probos / docili* and *placidae* and between *mores* and *quietem.* The working out of proper examples, and proper teaching, for Rome's young can only lead to calm and quiet for the aged. The suppressed implication is that in their absence only trouble and unrest can result. The poem itself, delivered by a *doctus chorus* (75), incorporates and projects the potential of good teaching, among other virtues, to make abstracts concrete and vice versa.

53. Although Romulus enters the poem at an appropriate chronological moment between Aeneas and Augustus, and as an obvious way station between the two as another of Rome's founders, he does not carry the intellectual weight allotted by Horace to the others. We may speculate on the reasons but one would doubtless have occurred to a Roman reader. Both Romulus and Augustus were interested in maintaining and enhancing Rome's population. Romulus resorted to violence to gain his ends, Augustus only to the force of law (and to the potential of priests and a poet).

54. The hypermetric line 47 may be meant to complement the (super)-abundance of Rome's blessings outlined in the stanza as a whole.

55. Zosimus 2. 6. 16–18.

56. The same elegy of Propertius that describes the Danaid portico and the adjoining temple to Apollo also informs us that the altar in front of it had as adornment on four sides statues of bulls, "living signs" (*vivida signa,* Prop. 2. 31. 8), by the sculptor Myron. Once more Horace may wish us to share visually in the proceedings as, at least according to the poem, we anticipate Augustus' offering of white bulls on an altar with four of the same animals embellishing it.

57. Pl. *Rud.* 305.

58. *C.* 4. 14. 52, 4. 15. 32.

59. *Parcere subiectis et debellare superbos* (*Aen.* 6. 853). It is a brilliant aperçu of Feeney (1998), 36, that Horace is alluding to the language of the Sibylline oracle (Zosimus 2. 6. 3), announcing the need for *Ludi* with the command "O Roman, remember." The language clearly parallels Anchises' to his son as he begins his crucial peroration (*Aen.* 6. 851): *"Romane, memento."*

60. Lines 50–51 may also cause us to remember an earlier moment in Anchises' speech where *prior* and *sanguis* appear in adjacent lines (852–53). On this occasion the words refer to the restraint that Anchises prays Julius Caesar, Augustus' great-uncle and adoptive father, will practice.

61. *Aen.* 7. 602, 604–6.

62. *Aen.* 1. 7.

63. On the nuances of the phrase *responsa petunt* and its various interpretations, see Fraenkel 376, n. 4. We can compare Virgil's language at *Aen.* 6. 798–99 where Anchises, in the role of prophet, predicts the time when Augustus, incorporating the might of Rome, will journey against her eastern enemies. At his advent kings around the Caspian and Lake Maeotis "shudder at the responses of the gods" (*responsis horrent divum*). In Horace's new vision, Rome itself has become the oracular divinity.

64. *Aen.* 6. 878.

65. Williams (1968), 59.

66. See, for instance, Tellus with twins and Cornucopia on the statue of Augustus from Prima Porta (as illustrated in Zanker, 180 and 193–94, in Shapiro, trans., 176 and 190–91).

67. The word *adparet*, with the overtones of magic we have noted, strongly supports the poet's apocalyptic tone as his song first personifies immortal abstractions crucial for Rome's well-being and then elicits and reveals their immortal presences.

68. At 68 I follow the text of Klingner and adopt (and translate) *prorogat* over *proroget* (which has equally strong manuscript authority) as forming suitable balance and parallel grammatical mood to *curat* (71) and *adplicat* (72), which are the universal readings.

69. It is not the case, as Fraenkel claims (372), that Apollo receives the lion's share of the poem ("It is Apollo, and not his sister, who remains the leading partner throughout"). Horace is careful not only to offer his celestial addressees equal amounts of the ode but to maintain a balance between male and female throughout, not only between Apollo and Diana (and their attributes, *Sol* and *Luna*) and between the equal-numbered choruses but also, to offer only select examples, between human mothers and

fathers, between the divine protectors Ceres and Tellus, on the one hand, and Jupiter, on the other. The union between Anchises and Venus (50), in such a context, takes on the quality of paradigm.

70. For detailed commentary on the symbolism of Apollo's relinquishment of the bow in favor of the lyre, see P. Fedeli, ed., *Properzio: Elegie: Libro IV* (Bari, 1965), on 4. 6., 69-70.

71. Festus 310-12L. See L. Richardson, Jr., *A New Topographical Dictionary of Ancient Rome* (Baltimore, 1992), s.v. "Roma Quadrata," 333, who summarizes: "a shrine on the Palatine . . . in which were deposited those things used to found a city auspiciously." The connection of the Auguratorium, where Romulus presumably took his founding auspices, with the shrine of Roma Quadrata and the *area Apollinis* is confirmed by F. Coarelli *Roma* (Bari, 1995), 162.

72. Suet. *Aug.* 7; Enn. *Ann.* 155S.

73. On Romulus as augur, see Enn. *Ann.* 73S

74. Prop. 2. 31. 5-6, 15-16. On the first statue see H. Last, "The *Tabula Hebana* and Propertius II, 31," *JRS* 43 (1953): 27-29.

75. *Epi.* 1. 3. 17.

76. . . . *si munus Apolline dignum / vis complere libris (epi.* 2. 1. 216-17).

77. . . . *vacuam Romanis vatibus aedem (epi.* 2. 2. 94). The dating of the two long epistles remains in question but the second, by disavowing lyric poetry in favor of philosophy in a manner that resembles the opening of the first epistle of book 1 (with *epi.* 2. 2. 141-44 cf. *epi.* 1. 1. 10-12), would seem to precede Horace's resumption of the writing of lyric verse, and therefore the composition of the *Carmen,* while the first, with its clear reference to the *Carmen* at 132-38, certainly follows its performance. See chap. 7, n. 1.

78. For the temple, see Zanker, 74-75 and 94, in Shapiro, trans., 66-69 and 89. For the stage performances, *CIL* 6. 32323. 157-58.

79. Cf. *CIL* 6. 32323. 150.

80. The repetitions of the *Ludi* are a prime example of "secularity." See chap. 7 for a detailed discussion of their earlier celebration.

Occurrences of the games are listed by Censorinus (*DN* 10-11). Dio Cassius (54. 18), in his survey of the year 17, states that Augustus' *Ludi* were the fifth such celebration (see also chap. 2, n. 67). The evidence is collected by Pighi and summarized by L. R. Taylor (*OCD*, 2d ed., s.v. "Secular Games") and W. Gross (*Der Kleine Pauly* 4. 1493, s.v. *saeculum*). On the performance of 348 see, L. R. Taylor, "New Light on the History of the Secular Games," *AJP* 55 (1934): 101-20; MacBain, 34.

81. It is, of course, possible that *puerorum* (71) might include the girls as well as the boys, but, at least at 6 and 34–36 Horace is explicit about the differentiation.

82. A list of verbal parallels between the poem's beginning and end is useful: *dicere carmen* (8), *dicere laudes* (76); *precamur* (3), *preces* (70); *semper* (3), *semper* (67); *pueros* (6), *puerorum* (71).

83. On two occasions the poem comes close to revealing the teacher-poet's presence and to speak directly though him. The first is at 33–36 where, especially in the light of *precamur* (3), the absence of the first person is striking. We expect: "Apollo hear *us*, suppliant boys, and Luna *us*, suppliant girls." Instead the suppression of the first person gives the sense of the poet commanding the gods to hear the double chorus as it sings.

The second is at 61–72 where the dispassion of third person narrative offers the impression that we have a detached speaker telling the tale of what first Apollo, then Diana does, as she "applies friendly ears to the prayers of the boys." It is as if we were learning at secondhand what Diana's intentions were rather than hearing the chorus directly pronounce on the effects of its prayerful chants.

Given the practicalities of the situation, i.e., an inscription that tells us directly *Carmen composuit Q. Horatius Flaccus*, we have more right than in most other lyric situations to draw an intimate connection between speaking voice and poet-creator of that voice.

84. In this context, the mention of Jupiter (73) is especially striking, given the fact that he is never named, not to say specifically addressed, elsewhere in the *Carmen*.

CHAPTER 4
Horatian Hymn and the *Carmen Saeculare*

1. On the possibility of choric divisions, see esp. Landmann. The odd number of stanzas could be explained by the two choruses coming together at the end for the last quatrain. But there arises the immediate difficulty of assigning the three preceding stanzas, two of which are allotted to Apollo but only one to Diana.

2. I agree with the majority of critics who place the publication of *Odes* 4 in the year 13. See Putnam (1986), passim, and, most recently, Habinek, 196–97, n. 5.

3. For a detailed discussion of the interrelationship of *c.* 4. 6, Pindar's sixth *Paean,* and the *Carmen,* see Hardie (1998).

4. I add this proviso because, from the beginning of his epic but with

particular intensity in its last three books, Virgil is at pains to draw connections between Achilles and Aeneas.

5. *Aen.* 8. 704–6.

CHAPTER 5

Horace and the Hellenic Heritage

1. The translation is by W. Race from *Pindar:* II (Loeb Classical Library: Cambridge, 1997) whose text my paraphrases also follow.

2. For a palinode on Pindar's part, apparently in response to his treatment of Neoptolemus here, cf. *Nem.* 7. 34–38, 102–4. A. P. Burnett (*Revenge in Attic and Later Tragedy* [Berkeley, 1998]) offers a comprehensive review of the idea of reprisal in Greek tragedy.

3. On the text of *Paean* 6, see now I. Rutherford, "For the Aeiginetans to Aiakos a Prosodion: An Unnoticed Title at Pindar, Paean 6, 123 and Its Significance for the Poem," *ZPE* 118 (1997): 1–21.

4. We must note here the importance of Simonides *eleg.* fr. 11. 1–12 (M. West, ed., *Iambi et Elegi Graeci*, 2d ed. [Oxford, 1992]) for both *c.* 4. 6 and the *Carmen*. The connection has been discussed with care and sensitivity by Barchiesi (1995). He well illustrates, through analysis of Horace's double bow in *c.* 4. 6 to Homer and Simonides, the change from the Greek poet's praise of Achilles (because he was slain only at the hand of a god) to Horace's *elogium* of Apollo (who fells the monstrous warrior bent on eradicating all Trojans). Apollo's violence is suppressed in the *Carmen*, but the strong connection of it with *c.* 4. 6 reminds us, as Barchiesi observes (37), that without Achilles' death there would have been no Troy to suffer metamorphosis into Rome.

    For the more general influence of Simonides on the fourth book of odes, see Barchiesi (1996). Of particular importance for our discussion is section 2: "Pindar and Simonides: Influence on 4. 6," 8–11.

5. The relationship of Horace and the Greek lyric poets has been treated most recently by Feeney (1993).

6. I am speaking only in general terms. Horace can use Sapphics for poems with prominently public themes (e.g., *c.* 1. 2 and 1. 12) just as he can opt for Alcaics when dealing with private matters, as in the cases of *c.* 1. 17 and 2. 11.

7. As noted above, it is important to remember that Horace's first two political odes (*c.* 1. 2 and 1. 12) are written in Sapphics. Because these are among Horace's main precedents as he writes the *Carmen*, two of the poet's chief purposes in adopting the meter for his public poem would

be both to complement and to respond to their contents. To the paranoia of *c.* 1. 2, the *Carmen* offers the probability of moral steadiness in state and statesman, and *c.* 1. 12 ends with one of the poet's several "lectures" to Augustus. If *c.* 3. 4 expounds to the emperor a mythic precedent for behavior when he finds himself omnipotent, *c.* 1. 12 is a clear rejoinder to him that, whatever power may come his way, "he will justly rule the wide earth subordinate to you [Jupiter]" (*c.* 1. 12. 57). In the *Carmen,* future has become present and *lenitas* a mark of Augustus' ongoing rule.

On the use of Sapphics for political poetry, see Nisbet and Hubbard, 20 (on *c.* 1. 2, intro.).

8. The *Carmen* may document a post-epic moment but, ironically, Ennius' *Annales,* as well as the *Aeneid,* is also a source for Horace here. With the phrase *remque Romanam Latiumque felix* (66) cf. *Ann.* 496S (*rem Romanam Latiumque*). Kiessling and Heinze also rightly refer to *Ann.* 109S — *tu produxisti nos intra luminis oras* — in connection with the use of *produco* at *C. S.* 17. But we remain insufficiently informed in any depth about either Ennian context to pass assured judgment on the purposes of Horace's borrowings.

9. In this context, however, it is well to note that the addition of twenty-seven boys to the chorus may be a novelty of the *Ludi* of 17 (Fraenkel 380–81, n. 3). If Apollo and Diana are almost equally balanced in the poet's treatment throughout the *Carmen,* so are the number of performers by sex.

10. See below on *epi.* 2. 1. 132–38 and Horace's boast of a public role as implementer of his song.

11. We may presume, however, that a text of the ode in his honor was sent or delivered by Pindar to the victor (or patron) whom he was celebrating.

12. On Pindar and Horace, see Highbarger; Fraenkel, 432–40; Kennedy; Freis; Feeney (1993), 43, 53; Lowrie, 70–76.

13. This is not to say that Pindar's myths cannot on occasion be historical. Cf. the foundation of Rhodes as described in *Ol.* 7, a poem, according to the scholiasts, inscribed in letters of gold within the temple of Athena at Lindos.

CHAPTER 6
The *Carmen Saeculare* and Latin Poetry

1. For a suggestion, see T. P. Wiseman, *Catullus and His World: A Reappraisal* (Cambridge, 1985), 98–99, 199.

2. Cat. 34. 21–22. Horace does use the phrase at *c.* 3. 21. 5 as part of his parodic hymn to the wine jug.

3. Horace picks up Catullus' use of *frugibus* (20) with *frugum* (29).

4. Cat. 64. 306.

5. Cat. 64. 321–22.

6. The allusion is noted by Kiessling and Heinze (on l. 57) who, though they agree that Horace might wish his hearers to have a sense of a golden era renewed under Augustus, dilute their comment with a proviso: "aber mythisch-poetische Phantasien, wie sie Virgil in der 4. Ekloge vorträgt, liegen unserem Liede fern, ebenso fern, wie dem Virgil der Gedanke an römische Säkularrechnung gelegen hat."

7. *Ecl.* 4. 6.

8. Ara. *Ph.* 133–36. The phrase *patriis virtutibus* is present some ten lines later in *ecl.* 4 (17) and the abstract *virtus* at 27.

9. Virgil uses *nascor* three times (5, 8 and 25). We have *suboles* at *ecl.* 4. 49; *subolem* at *C. S.* 17.

10. For one verbal instance, Virgil uses *aevum* at *ecl.* 4. 11, Horace at *C. S.* 68.

11. Diana: *ecl.* 4. 10, *C. S.* 15. It is not coincidental that Servius, in his commentary on *eclogue* 4, refers to the *Carmen* on three occasions (on lines 5, 10, and 47) to gloss his own material.

12. *Decus: ecl.* 4. 11; *C. S.* 2, 48, and 61. Fertility of Tellus: *ecl.* 4. 19, and 39, *C. S.* 29 — all at line endings.

13. *Ecl.* 4. 34–36.

14. By giving his poem a dramatic date of 40 B.C.E. but by not naming a specific child, not to mention assigning it parentage, Virgil plays with his reader and leaves the door open for continuing scholarly debate about who is meant. (In correspondence, Alessandro Barchiesi uses the phrase "pregnancy politics" to summarize Virgil's attitude toward those in power.)

    By the time of the performance of the *Ludi,* Augustus' only child, Julia, now married to Agrippa, had borne at least one and probably two male children, Gaius (born in 20) and Lucius (born sometime in 17). Although neither daughter nor grandchildren are mentioned in the *Carmen,* to honor Julia's fecundity would doubtless have been one of Augustus' reasons for celebrating the *Ludi* in the first place. Her name, after all, is shared with the *lex Iulia de maritandis ordinibus* of 18. (On the place of Gaius and Lucius in Augustus' iconographic program see Zanker 218–26, in Shapiro, trans. 215–23.)

15. *Aen.* 6. 851.

16. See also chap. 2, n. 59.

17. Other examples of the influence of Tibullus on the *Carmen* deserve separate study. Cf., e.g., Tib. 1. 1. 15–16 (*Ceres . . . corona / spicea*) with *C. S.* 30 (*spicea . . . Cererem corona*).

18. Since Tibullus' second book consists of only six poems, the last of which is inordinately brief, it was probably not complete at his death and was published, we presume, as he left it.

19. With *aras* and *sacra* (Tib. 2. 5. 6) cf. *C. S.* 4 (*tempore sacro*) and 65 (*Palatinas aras*).

20. Tibullus' Apollo *nitidus* (2. 5. 7) bears comparison with the Sun's bright chariot (*curru nitido*) at *C. S.* 9.

21. In Tibullus (2. 5. 11) an augur is beholden to Apollo; at *C. S.* 61 it is the god himself who is augur.

22. Tibullus' expansive reference to the Sibyl's hexameters (2. 5. 16, *senis pedibus*) Horace leaves simply as *Sibyllini versus* (5).

23. Tibullus' listing has close parallels to those of Virgil (*geo.* 1. 469–88) and Ovid (*M.* 15. 783–98), as well as of Plutarch, Appian, and Dio Cassius. For further details, see *Tibullus, Elegies II,* ed. P. Murgatroyd (Oxford, 1994), on 2. 5. 71–72.

24. Mention of the Palilia is another, final reminder that our inner eye should still remain concentrated on the Palatine. Cf. Palatia (25) and the ancient derivation (Solinus 1. 19) of Parilia (Palilia) from *partus Iliae,* a derivation apropos for the *Carmen* as well.

25. The resultant fertility, of mothers with offspring, is a theme common to both poems (with Tib. 2. 5. 91–94 cf. *C. S.* 13–16 and 31).

CHAPTER 7

The *Carmen Saeculare* and *Carmina*

1. On the dating, which most critics cogently place between 12 and 10, see *Horace: Epistles Book II and Epistle to the Pisones,* ed. N. Rudd (Cambridge, 1989), 1–2; Habinek, 196–97, n. 5.

2. *Epi.* 2. 1. 132–37.

3. The brusque play between *praesentia* and *sentit* may be meant to imitate the incantations which the chorus utters and of which the speaker tells.

4. See, most recently, P. Hardie (*Virgil: Aeneid: Book IX* [Cambridge, 1994]), on *Aen* 9. 774–78. Virgil draws on the assonantal connection, for example, at *ecl.* 1. 77 (*carmina nulla canam*), and we find *canamus, canimus,* and *carmen* within the first four lines of *ecl.* 4. For a survey of the various usages of *carmina* in literature of the early and middle Republican period,

see G. Williams in *Latin Literature,* vol. 2 of *The Cambridge History of Classical Literature* (Cambridge, 1982), 53–55.

For discussions of magic in the life and literature of Rome, see A.-M. Tupet, *La magie dans la poésie Latine* (Paris, 1976); G. Luck, *Arcana Mundi: Magic and the Occult in the Greek and Roman Worlds* (Baltimore, 1985); F. Graf, *Magic in the Ancient World* (Cambridge, 1997). More specifically, on the poetics of magic, see H. S. Versnel, "Die Poetik der Zaubersprüche" in *Die Macht des Wortes,* ed. T. Schabert and R. Brague (Munich, 1996), 233–97, and for analysis of a specialized example of magic in Virgilian poetry, C. Faraone, "Clay Hardens and Wax Melts: Magical Role-Reversal in Vergil's Eighth *Eclogue,*" *CP* 84 (1989): 296–97.

For a detailed discussion of the use of *cano* in Republican and Augustan poetry, see Newman (1965).

5. Pliny *HN* 28. 17; Aug. *CD* 2. 8 (quoting Cic. *RP* 4. 2). For a discussion of the various meanings of *mala carmina* and of the distinction between *bona* and *mala carmina* at Hor. *Sat.* 2. 1. 80–85, see LaFleur, 1816–17.

6. Seneca speaks of a prohibition "lest anyone 'sing away' another's crops" (*ne quis alienos fructus excantassit, NQ* 4. 7. 2), and Pliny of someone "who might 'sing away' crops" (*qui fruges excantassit, HN* 28. 17), both no doubt variations on the same theme. Cf. the different but illuminating language of Servius, on Vir. *ecl.* 8. 99, quoting a prohibition "lest you lure another's grain-crop" (*neve alienam segetem pellexeris*).

7. For detailed commentary on the early hymns, see E. Norden *Aus altrömischen Priesterbüchern* (Lund, 1939).

8. *Ecl.* 9. 10, 11–12.

9. On the word and its origins, see R. Coleman (*Vergil: Eclogues* [Cambridge, 1977]) on *ecl.* 7. 28. For Varro (*LL* 7. 36) the etymology is derived *a versibus viendis* ("from the plaiting of verses"). Cf. Isid. *orig.* 8. 7. 3.

10. Earlier in the poem, when proclaiming Phoebus Apollo as the source of his "art of song" (*artem carminis*), he attributes also to the god his "repute as poet" (*nomen poetae,* 29–30). When the Greek tradition of inspiration is foremost in his mind, Horace uses the word *poeta.* When Roman performance is the subject, *vatis* regularly becomes his title.

It is a matter of interest that, though Horace uses forms of *vatis* on six occasions, the word *poeta* never appears in the first collection of odes. (For a full survey of the meaning and usage of *vatis,* see Newman [1967].)

11. *Epi.* 2. 1. 138, 133.

12. Lucilius 567M.

13. *Ecl.* 8. 10. Cf. line 3 for the magic effect of the speaker's own "pastoral" *carmen.*

14. *Geo.* 4. 565 (defining the *Eclogues* themselves); *geo.* 2. 176, of the works of Hesiod.

15. For *carmen* in a specifically magical sense see, Prop. 1. 1. 24, 1. 18. 9, and 2. 28. 35 (*magico carmine*).

16. Virgil may be using the word *carminibus* here in irony—or even humor—since, as Denis Feeney points out to me, Oebalus is never mentioned again in the epic. The poet is possibly thinking of Homer's Nireus (*Iliad* 2. 671–75) who appears with astonishing rhetorical emphasis in the catalogue of ships but also never again. I have elsewhere suggested that he serves as a model for Umbro who is described not long after Oebalus in Virgil's catalogue of Latin heroes in *Aen.* 7 (750–60). (See Putnam [1995], 127–31.) The link may well be deliberate on the poet's part.

17. *Aen.* 9. 446–49.

18. Given mention of his delight in lyric poetry here, there is no reason why the reference to Florus' *amabile carmen* at *epi.* 1. 3. 24 should not also refer specifically to lyric verse.

19. We must not forget that Horace's only previous nonhexameter collection is entitled *Liber Epodon*, i.e., book of incantations (Luck, *Arcana Mundi*, 73).

20. Livy 7. 27. 1. See Taylor, "New Light," passim. For further details on the connection of pestilence with the origin of the games see, MacBain, 34 and n. 67.

21. Pseudo-Acro on Hor. *C. S.* 8, referring to Valerius [*sic*] Flaccus. We hear at the beginning of his gloss of the earlier *carmen saeculare* and at the end of "a song sung between the sacrifices" (*carmen cantatum inter sacrificia*).

22. On the attempts to connect Livius Andronicus with the *carmen* of 249, see M. von Albrecht, *A History of Roman Literature* (Leiden, 1997), I, 112, n. 3.

23. Livy *Periocha* 49; Censorinus *DN* 17. 11.

24. Livy 27. 37. 7. Shortly later the historian allows himself a negative comment on the song's style (27. 37. 13). Cf. Festus 446L for details on the honor bestowed on Livius at that time.

25. Livy 31. 12. 10. The wording of the historian's comment (*Carmen, sicut patrum memoria Livius, ita tum condidit P. Licinius Tegula*) suggests strongly that Livius was no longer among the quick. The Sibylline books had also been consulted in 217 in like circumstances, but no song is mentioned as part of the expiatory rites (Livy 22. 1. 16).

It should be said here that Augustus' consultation of the Sibylline books in 17 also marks a consequential departure from tradition, which regularly marks such consultations as occurring in moments of crisis. For a succinct piece of evidence, note Dio. Hal. 44. 62. 5: "[The Romans] consult [the Sibylline oracles] by order of the senate, when the state is in the grip of party strife or some great misfortune has happened to them in war, or some important prodigies and apparitions have been seen which are difficult of interpretation, as has often happened." See also Livy 10. 8. 2 and, for further details, Smith, 444 (intro. to Tib. 2. 5), referring especially to Cic. *Div.* 2. 112, et al.; Murgatroyd, ed., *Tibullus, Elegies II,* 163-64 (intro. to Tib. 2. 5).

On the *Quindecimviri,* see A. A. Boyce "The Development of the *Decemviri sacris faciundis,*" *TAPA* 69 (1038): 161-87, and *RE* 24 (1963): 1114-48 s.v. *Quindecimviri* (G. Radke). There is full discussion of both the sibyls and their prophecies in Parke.

26. *Prodigiorum Libri,* ed. O. Rossbach (Leipzig, 1910), 162-63, under the years 119 and 117.

27. Tib. 2. 5. 79-80.

28. There is also a plethora of further repetitions that, by their superimpositions and interlarding, give the poem often the semblance of a palimpsest. The phrase *urbe Roma* (11) is carefully echoed in *Roma* (37) and *urbem* (39) as the ode's second segment commences (see Arnold, 481-82, for this and other parallel echoes). Likewise *prolis* (19) is picked up with *prolem* (47) as the generalized youth of Rome's generativeness become the specific Romans on whose behalf the chorus prays. Among other repetitions, some already noted, we might list: *castos* (6), *castus* (42); *lenis* (14, 52); *decus* (2, 48, and n.b. *decorus,* 61); *rerum* (26), *rem* (47), *rem* (66); *potens* (1), *potentis* (53); *date* (3), *daturus* (43), *date* (47); *placidus* (33), *placidae* (46); *iam* (27, 53, 55, 57).

29. Such linearity reinforces the essentially public aspect of the Carmen just as it reminds us of the universality of Rome and its empire at large. But this comprehensiveness finds proper counterpoise in the circularity of the poem, which mentions of the Palatine and several other verbal parallels at the beginning and the end abet. Such a lexical embrace suggests that the very openness of the poem helps define a more intimate, sequestered side that focuses on fifty-four young people chanting to the gods from a particular part of one of Rome's central hills. The poem's rounded compass metaphorically encloses the city near to hand and reminds us that it is from her present and future citizenry, and their special ceremonials, that her greatness will continue to stem.

Select Bibliography

Ableitinger, D. "Die Aeneassage im Carmen Saeculare des Horaz (Verse 37–44)," *WS* 6 (1972): 33–44.

Arnold, B. "A Reevaluation of the Artistry of Horace's *Carmen Saeculare*," in *Studies in Latin Literature and Roman History*, vol. 4, ed. C. Deroux, *Collection Latomus* 196 (Brussels, 1986), 475–91.

Barchiesi, A. *Il poeta e il principe: Ovidio e il discorso augusteo* (Bari, 1994). Trans. as *The Poet and the Prince: Ovid and Augustan Discourse* (Berkeley, 1997).

———. "Simonides e Orazio sulla morte di Achille," *ZPE* 107 (1995): 33–38.

———. "Poetry, Praise and Patronage: Simonides in Book 4 of Horace's *Odes*," *CA* 15 (1996): 5–47.

Barker, D. "'The Golden Age Is Proclaimed?' The *Carmen Saeculare* and the Renascence of the Golden Race," *CQ* 46 (1996): 434–46.

Collinge, N. *The Structure of Horace's Odes* (Oxford, 1961).

Commager, S. *The Odes of Horace* (New Haven, 1962).

Davis, G. *Polyhymnia: The Rhetoric of Horatian Lyric Discourse* (Berkeley, 1991).

Doblhofer, E. *Horaz in der Forschung nach 1957, Erträge der Forschung* 279 (Darmstadt, 1992).

Feeney, D. "Horace and the Greek Lyric Poets," in *Horace 2000: A Celebration*, ed. N. Rudd (Ann Arbor, 1993), 41–63.

———. *Literature and Religion at Rome: Culture, Contexts, and Beliefs* (Cambridge, 1998).

Fitzgerald, W. "Horace, Pleasure and the Text," *Arethusa* 22 (1989): 81–103.

Fowler, W. W. "The Carmen Saeculare of Horace and Its Performance, June 3 B.C. 17," *CQ* 4 (1910): 148.

Fraenkel, H. *Horace* (Oxford, 1957).

Freis, R. "The Catalogue of Pindaric Genres in Horace *Ode* 4.2," *CA* 2 (1983): 27–36.

Gagé, J. "Observations sur le Carmen Saeculare d'Horace," *REL* 9 (1931): 307.

Galinsky, K. "Sol and the Carmen Saeculare," *Latomus* 26 (1967): 619-33.

———. *Augustan Culture: An Interpretive Introduction* (Princeton, 1996).

Habinek, T. *The Politics of Latin Literature* (Princeton, 1998).

Hardie, A. "Horace, the Paean and Roman Choreia (*Odes* 4. 6)," *PLLS* 10 (1998): 251-93.

Hardie, P. "*Ut pictura poesis?* Horace and the Visual Arts," in *Horace 2000: A Celebration,* ed. N. Rudd (Ann Arbor, 1993), 120-39.

Highbarger, E. L. "The Pindaric Style of Horace," *TAPA* 66 (1935): 222-55.

Iwasaki, T. "Apollo and Diana in Horace's Carmen Saeculare," *JCS* 33 (1985): 80-87.

Kennedy, N. T. "Pindar and Horace," *AC* 18 (1975): 9-24.

Kiessling, A., and R. Heinze, eds., *Q. Horatius Flaccus: Oden und Epoden* (Zurich, 1968).

LaFleur, R. "Horace and *Onomasti Komodein:* The Law of Satire," *ANRW* 2.31.3 (1981): 1790-1826.

Landmann, M. "Die Aufteilung der Chöre im Carmen Saeculare," *Aparchai* 4 (1961): 179.

La Penna, A. *Orazio e l'ideologia del principato* (Turin, 1963).

Latte, K. *Römische Religionsgeschichte* (Munich, 1960).

Lowrie, M. *Horace's Narrative Odes* (Oxford, 1997).

Lyne, R. O. A. M. *Horace: Behind the Public Poetry* (New Haven, 1995).

MacBain, B. *Prodigy and Expiation: A Study in Religion and Politics in Republican Rome, Collection Latomus* 177 (Brussels, 1982).

Manfredini, A. "Il Carmen saeculare di Orazio," *RSC* 27 (1979): 406-30.

McDermott, E. A. "Greek and Roman Elements in Horace's Lyric Program," *ANRW* 2.31.2 (1981): 1640-72.

Menozzi, E. "La composizione strofica des Carmen Saeculare," *SIFC* 13 (1905): 67-73.

Miller, P. A. *Lyric Texts and Lyric Consciousness* (London, 1994).

Mommsen, T. "Die Akten zu dem Säkulargedicht des Horaz," in *Reden und Aufsätze* (Berlin, 1905), 351-59.

Newman, J. K. "De verbis *canere* et *dicere* eorumque apud poetas latinos ab Ennio usque ad aetatem Augusti usu," *Latinitas* 13 (1965): 86-106. Trans. and rev. in *Roman Catullus and the Modification of the Alexandrian Sensibility* (Hildesheim, 1990), app. 2, 422-34.

———. *The Concept of Vatès in Augustan Poetry, Collection Latomus* 89 (Brussels, 1967).

Nilsson, M. P. "Saeculares Ludi," *RE* 2.IA.2 (1920): 1696-1720.

Nisbet, R. G. M., and M. Hubbard. *A Commentary on Horace: Odes: Book I* (Oxford, 1970).

Oliensis, E. *Horace and the Rhetoric of Authority* (Cambridge, 1998).

Parke, H. W. *Sibyls and Sibylline Prophecy in Classical Antiquity* (London, 1988).

Pighi, G. B. *De Ludis Saecularibus P. R. Quiritium* (Amsterdam, 1965).

Putnam, M. C. J. "Horace C. 3. 30: The Lyricist as Hero," *Ramus* 22 (1973): 1–19. Repr. in *Essays on Latin Lyric, Elegy, and Epic* (Princeton, 1982), 133–5.

——. *Artifices of Eternity: Horace's Fourth Book of Odes* (Ithaca, 1986).

——. *Virgil's Aeneid: Interpretation and Influence* (Chapel Hill, 1995).

——. "Horace *c.* 3. 23: Ritual as Art," in *Rome and Her Monuments: Essays on the City and Literature of Rome in Honor of Katherine Geffcken*, ed. S. Dickison and J. Hallett (Wauconda, 2000).

Radke, G. "Aspetti religiosi ed elementi politici nel Carmen Saeculare," *RCCM* 20 (1978): 1093–1116.

——, and S. Mariotti. "Carme secolare," in *Enciclopedia Oraziana* (Rome, 1996), 300–3.

Rahn, H. "Zum Carmen Saeculare des Horaz," *Gymnasium* 77 (1970): 467–79.

Reckford, K. *Horace* (New York, 1969).

Redslob, E. *Kritische Bemerkungen zu Horaz* (Weimar, 1912).

Santirocco, M. *Unity and Design in Horace's Odes* (Chapel Hill, 1986).

Schmidt, P. L. "Horaz' Säkulargedicht—ein Prozessionslied?" *AU* 28 (1985): 42–53.

Vahlen, J. "Über das Säkulargedicht des Horatius," *Sitz. Berlin* (1892), 1015–16. Repr. in *Gesammelte Philologische Schriften*, vol. 2 (Leipzig and Berlin, 1923), 380–81.

White, P. *Promised Verse: Poets in the Society of Augustan Rome* (Cambridge, 1993).

Williams, G. *Tradition and Originality in Roman Poetry* (Oxford, 1968).

——. *The Third Book of Horace's Odes* (Oxford, 1969).

——. *Horace*, vol. 6 of *Greece and Rome: New Surveys in the Classics* (Oxford, 1972).

Woodman, A. J. "*Exegi monumentum:* Horace, *Odes* 3. 30," in A. J. Woodman and D. West, eds., *Quality and Pleasure in Latin Poetry* (Cambridge, 1974), 115–28 and 151–56.

Zanker, P. *Augustus und die Macht der Bilder* (Munich, 1987). Trans. A. Shapiro, as *The Power of Images in the Age of Augustus* (Ann Arbor, 1988).

INDEX

2004, 02, 03 B   30,00 (12,98)